STO

ACPL

DISCARDED

Sinclair, Carole.

Keys to women's basic
professional services

KEYS
TO WOMEN'S BASIC
PROFESSIONAL
NEEDS

Carole Sinclair
Publishing Executive

BARRON'S

Allen County Public Library
900 Webster Street
PO Box 2270
Fort Wayne, IN 46801-2270

© Copyright 1991 by Carole Sinclair

All rights reserved.
No part of this book may be reproduced
in any form, by photostat, microfilm, xerography,
or any other means, or incorporated into any
information retrieval system, electronic or
mechanical, without the written permission
of the copyright owner.

All inquiries should be addressed to:
Barron's Educational Series, Inc.
250 Wireless Boulevard
Hauppauge, New York 11788

Library of Congress Catalog Card Number 91-9539

International Standard Book No. 0-8120-4608-0

Library of Congress Cataloging in Publication Data

Sinclair, Carole.
  Keys to women's basic professional needs / by Carole Sinclair.
       p.   cm.—(Barron's business keys)
    Includes index.
    ISBN 0-8120-4608-0
    1. Women—Finance, Personal.   2. Women—Vocational
guidance.
    I. Title. II. Series.
HG179.S49 1991
332.024′042—dc20   91-9539
                                                        CIP

PRINTED IN THE UNITED STATES OF AMERICA
1234   5500   987654321

Dedication

For my daughter, Wendy, with love.

Acknowledgements

I wish to offer special thanks to my friend and business partner Sylvia Porter, who inspired me. To Caroline Urbas whose support and contribution have been significant, and to my editor, Jane O'Sullivan.

To my accountant, David Kahn, to my insurance broker DeWitt Stern, and to my lawyer Alan Hartnick for their professional advice.

Disclaimer

This information is intended to provide general information and background and is distributed on the basis that the publisher and copyright owner are not engaged in rendering legal, accounting or other professional services.

Should legal, accounting or other professional assistance be required the services of a competent professional should be sought.

The publisher, copyright owner, and authors disclaim any personal liability for advice or information presented herein.

CONTENTS

INTRODUCTION

As a contemporary woman, you are part of a transitional generation and, as with all things in transition, you have no clear guideposts to follow. Generations of women preceding yours relied on their husbands and families for financial advice and guidance; they were for the most part financially dependent and financially uneducated. The generation that will come after you, on the other hand, is independent, financially savvy, and able to take charge of its financial affairs early on. Today, girls in high school and college have specific financial and professional goals. These girls and young women expect to assume responsibility for their own financial existence and possibly that of dependents, and they make sure they have the proper tools to accomplish this. At a relatively young age they become familiar with the kinds of professional advisers who have always counseled men—accountants, bankers, lawyers, financial planners, insurance brokers, real estate brokers, and investment advisers. Many of these young women have no intention of leaving the work force, primarily for psychological reasons. They believe they will be happy in their work, and they see no reason to stop working until they are forced to by age or disability.

The older generation of women experienced relatively little change as they entered the "retirement" years. These women really didn't retire. Their main responsibilities had always been home, husband, and children, and, even as their husbands retired, they continued to perform most of the duties they always had. The concept of retirement planning for women, consequently, is relatively new. While most of the principles that work for men apply equally to women, there is one significant

1

difference. Women have traditionally cared for their children, their aging parents, and even their aging spouses. There is little evidence that this has changed. Consequently, women of retirement age face not only the financial changes and difficulties of retirement but an ever-increasing human burden as well. As a result, the issue of time management, which is at the front of many women's minds, continues to be important as women contemplate their retirement.

1

WHERE YOU ARE NOW

Women as a group are more independent today than they were in the past, some by choice and some by dint of necessity. Some are career women who have been in the work force for many years; these women are accustomed to getting a paycheck, paying their bills, paying taxes, handling employee benefits, and planning for retirement.

Some have spent many years as homemakers, leaving business and financial matters to their husbands. Many of these women unexpectedly find themselves "independent" as the result of divorce or separation.

Finally, because their average lifespan far exceeds that of men, many women outlive their husbands by one, two, or even three decades and are forced, frequently with no former experience, to take charge of their own business and financial matters.

Wherever you fit into this paradigm, your basic professional needs are the same. First, you need to determine for whom you have responsibility: yourself, possibly dependent children, possibly a spouse, possibly dependent parents. You must then consider your current economic status—whether you are employed full-time, employed part-time, looking for employment, or retired.

You should also review your financial standing—your savings and liquid assets; your real estate holdings and responsibilities; your debt; and your insurance coverage (health, disability, life, and property).

Do you have a will? If so, what is the status of your executor? Have you any trusts in place?

Finally, you should think through your retirement needs. Your years in retirement may exceed your years of employment. What expenses are you likely to face? What assets, savings, and benefit payments do you have to offset these expenses?

This analysis shows you where you are. Now consider where you want to be, in both the immediate and distant future. Are you on the right track, or will something have to change in order for you to meet your goals? Some of the planning you can do yourself, but professional advice may well be useful.

2

FINANCIAL PLANNING FOR A LIFETIME

Most professional women have studied the basic principles of financial planning in high school, college, or graduate school. No matter what level of sophistication you have achieved, you should begin a program of lifetime financial planning no later than the first day of your first employment.

Lifetime financial planning is a matter of setting short-term and long-term goals, putting price tags on them, and setting timetables. For instance, as a young professional or recent graduate, your short-term goals may be repaying educational loans, saving 5 percent of your gross income for retirement, and funding basic furniture needs. Longer-term goals might include saving the down payment for a first apartment or house or a car.

Lifetime financial planning is just that—a lifetime activity that should be reassessed at least yearly and preferably quarterly.

As you develop short- and long-range financial goals, you should assess your current and projected future earning power. You may need to decide whether to seek additional education in order to achieve a higher income.

Early in your career, debt should be kept to an absolute minimum; later, you may choose to take on reasonable and manageable debt for housing, investments, education, and support of dependents.

3

WHAT IS FINANCIAL PLANNING?

Financial planning is planning your financial life rather than taking it as it comes and being prepared for financial events rather than simply reacting to them.

To begin your own financial planning, list your assets and liabilities to create your net worth statement. Second, list all of your investments and their current and projected future return. Third, list all benefits you enjoy, including employee benefits such as health insurance, life insurance, low-interest loans, profit sharing, and stock options. Try also to estimate your future income from your current employment, whether you are working part-time or full-time, for someone else or for yourself.

To help with your retirement planning, you can find out what your Social Security benefits are likely to be. You can get a PEBES form from the Social Security office. This asks for your estimate of your future earnings and your expected age at retirement. Send this in, and the Social Security Administration will send you back an estimate of your benefits at retirement, based on your projections and your past history. You may want to do this regularly, especially as retirement nears, since benefits change.

Next, you should estimate your ongoing expenses. Work out a monthly budget that includes fixed expenses such as taxes, mortgage, insurance, tuition, and car payments, as well as other predictable expenses, such as food, clothing, vacations, and gifts. List on separate pages each significant expense you expect to incur in the future, such as tuition, mortgage, car, major trip, retirement (discussed in depth later in the book), and care of dependents; you will use these worksheets to help you plan how best to fund these expenses (see Key 5).

Estimate the amount you hope to save currently and in the future. Americans in general save a smaller percentage of income than do residents of other industrialized countries, which hurts everyone, individually and collectively. Try to get into the habit of saving something, beginning with your first job, even if it's a small amount.

4

YOUR SAVINGS AND
INVESTING NEEDS

Unless your money is working for you, earning interest or appreciating in an investment, you are actually losing money. Your money has to be active enough to stay ahead of the current and foreseeable rate of inflation. You can see from the chart in Key 7 what happens to your dollar if you "tuck it under the mattress." Saving is a habit you should start with your first job, putting away perhaps 5 percent of each paycheck. If you never touch your savings and they benefit from compounded interest, you will have a nice nest egg by the time you are in your thirties.

Money for investing should be set aside after you have taken care of projected savings, projected taxes, and projected day-to-day and fixed expenses. The first thing you should consider is how much risk you are comfortable with. Investments almost always carry some risk that you will lose all or some of your money. You may find that level of risk absolutely unacceptable for all your money but feel perfectly comfortable with a mix of investments in which 60 or 70 percent of your investment funds is conservatively invested, with little risk of a loss, and 25 or 30 percent is put into moderate- or high-risk investments that have the possibility of a better rate of return.

Your banker, your stockbroker, your lawyer, and your accountant will all try to advise you regarding investments, but in the end you have to decide how much risk you can live with. If you are a truly fearless type, willing to risk everything for the big return, you might consider putting 50 percent of your dollars in high-risk investments.

However, you should still keep a significant portion of your money in moderate- to low-risk vehicles to minimize the possibility of losing everything.

If you majored in economics at college and are in the finance field, by all means handle your investments yourself. If you are almost anyone else, chances are you would do better by investing in mutual funds, which are professionally managed and which always diversify. You might invest in several mutual funds, perhaps one high-risk, one moderate-risk, and one low-risk; within each of these mutual funds, the fund manager will diversify further. Ask your broker and other professional advisors to recommend mutual funds that best suit your investment strategy; in addition, all major financial newspapers and magazines carry listings of available mutual funds, including their special characteristics, and information about where to call or write for further information.

If you insist on managing a piece of your investing yourself, invest in something you know and understand. For instance, if you know computers, it will be easier for you to monitor the goings-on in that field and to track the performance of the companies in it. You should research all investments thoroughly and then monitor them carefully. It is a mistake to try to get in and out of the stock market quickly on your own; you will simply run up a lot of brokerage charges and possibly lose your money. If, on the other hand, you believe in a certain product or field and want to invest for the long term, it can be interesting for you to handle such an investment and to monitor it, reading annual reports, trade publications, even visiting the companies in which you are interested. This is the way mutual fund managers handle their investments; in order to have any chance of doing as well as they do, you need to be as thorough as they are.

5

REVIEWING CURRENT SPENDING PATTERNS

In addition to working out the funding necessary for future financial goals, you owe it to yourself to review your spending habits at least once a year. Perhaps you are spending too much on consumer loan interest, rent, car payments, or entertainment and travel. Review other ways of handling these expenses. For instance, perhaps you would be better off making a down payment on a modest house and making mortgage payments while you build equity in the house, rather than renting the house. Or perhaps you're currently spending a great deal on car payments when you would be better off leasing a car, especially if you are entitled to a partial income tax deduction for business use of an automobile.

Maintaining a Positive Cash Flow. At least twice a year you should review your real cash flow. You may be surprised at the results; income and expenses can become somewhat blurred because of the ready availability of credit.

If you find that you have a negative cash flow—that is, your expenses exceed your income—you should track your costs and income and make the changes necessary to bring it into line. Having a negative cash flow means that you are not financially healthy and are in no position to invest.

On the following page is a simple format for your use:

3 1833 02548 1547

Income
Salary and commissions _____
Social Security _____
Interest and dividends _____
Profits from business enterprises _____
Miscellaneous fees and royalties _____
Alimony and/or child support _____
Other _____
                                Total _____

Expenses
Monthly living expenses:
  Rent _____
  Household maintenance _____
  Utilities _____
  Insurance _____
  Transportation _____
  Food _____
  Clothing _____
  Medical _____
  Education _____
  Personal _____
  Savings _____
Debt obligations:
  Mortgage _____
  Principal and interest on bank debt _____
  Principal and interest on credit _____
  card debt
  Investment loans _____
Taxes:
  Federal _____
  State and local _____
  Social Security _____
  Real estate _____
                                Total _____

Total your annual income and annual expenses, and subtract the expense line from the income line. If there is a positive balance, you are in a position to invest. If, on the other hand, you have a negative cash flow, review each expense line and determine how much it can be cut back to bring your cash flow into line.

Emergency Fund. It's important that you establish an emergency fund equal to three to six months of necessary expenses, such as mortgage or rent, taxes, insurance, food, tuition, and car payments, to see you through an emergency or period of unemployment. This money should be liquid; in other words it should be readily accessible.

6

NET WORTH

To develop a net worth statement, list all your assets, along with their current market value. Classify the assets as liquid or nonliquid. Then list existing liabilities, that is, all debt, including your mortgage, tuition loans, credit card balances, and bank loans. If your liabilities exceed your assets, your first priority should be reducing your debt. If you are just breaking even or are unprepared for major future expenses, you need to plan to increase your income to cover these potential needs.

Preparing Your Personal Net Worth Statement. Your net worth is the difference between your total assets and your total liabilities. Potential lenders, investors, and partners will all want to review your net worth statement before proceeding in any business arrangement with you. The categories on the following page provide guidelines for preparing your statement.

Net Worth Statement

Assets

Residential real estate	_____
Furnishings	_____
Jewelry	_____
Furs	_____
Automobiles	_____
Boat	_____
Art	_____
Other collectibles	_____
Silver	_____
Cash on hand in savings	_____
Money market funds	_____
Certificates of deposit	_____
Cash value of life insurance	_____
Annuities	_____
Employee pension or benefit plan	_____
Stocks	_____
Bonds	_____
Mutual funds	_____
IRAs	_____
Keoghs	_____
Trust funds	_____
Business partnerships	_____
Total	_____

Liabilities

Mortgage	_____
Loans	_____
Installment account balances	_____
Taxes owed	_____
Total	_____
Total assets	_____
Minus Total liabilities	_____
Total net worth	_____

13

7

THE IMPACT OF INFLATION

Inflation—an increase in the cost of goods and services—undermines your net worth every minute of the day. No matter how much cash you have in the bank, no matter what the value of your investments, inflation eats away at the value of your savings every day. As the following chart demonstrates, if that process were to continue unchecked, your net worth would eventually be zero even if you never touched your capital.

One of your overriding financial objectives should be to stay ahead of inflation. Both your savings and investments must show an annual return greater than the annual inflation rate for you to be doing anything more than standing still or, worse yet, losing ground.

It is essential that you calculate the effect of inflation in your personal as well as business financial planning. The following chart shows you how the value of your dollar shrinks over the course of ten years at various rates of inflation:

THE EFFECT OF INFLATION ON YOUR DOLLAR

Years	5%	6%	7%	8%	9%	10%
1	95¢	94¢	94¢	93¢	92¢	91¢
2	91¢	89¢	87¢	86¢	84¢	83¢
3	86¢	84¢	82¢	79¢	77¢	75¢
4	82¢	79¢	76¢	74¢	71¢	68¢
5	78¢	75¢	71¢	68¢	65¢	62¢
6	75¢	71¢	67¢	63¢	60¢	56¢
7	71¢	67¢	62¢	58¢	55¢	51¢
8	68¢	63¢	58¢	54¢	50¢	47¢
9	65¢	59¢	54¢	50¢	46¢	42¢
10	61¢	56¢	51¢	46¢	42¢	39¢

8

FINANCIAL PLANNING FOR MAJOR GOALS

Review the worksheets you have made for those financial goals you expect to reach within five years, perhaps buying a new house or a new car. List the expense and the amount you will need to save between now and the date of the financial event in order to cover the expense. Alternatively, you may decide to borrow the money now and to repay it over a number of years, as with a mortgage. Calculate the cost both ways, and if at all possible save and pay cash for the item (a house is the exception to this rule because of the amount of money involved). If you borrow, although you obtain the item at once, you may find yourself saddled with payments, including very high interest costs, for years. The cost of borrowing the money to pay for one short-term financial goal may well equal the cost of achieving two goals with cash.

Finally, prepare worksheets for two or three long-range goals, for instance, your contribution to the support and care of an aging parent for ten or fifteen years. The sooner you make plans and start saving to cover important items such as this, the sooner you will work them into your daily financial life.

9

YOU AND YOUR CHILDREN

In addition to making a financial plan for yourself, you should also establish one for your child or children. Your child has medical needs, education needs, housing needs, and recreation needs, all of which should be anticipated.

First of all, you and your husband should select a guardian to raise your children if you both should die. The guardian need not be your best friend or closest relative. It should be someone in whose household your child's life would continue in a fashion most like that in your household. Similarities in child-raising beliefs and style, goals for higher education and religious education, money management, and health and fitness should all be considered, along with the obvious issues of who will love your child and who you believe to be most trustworthy.

If you will need day care for your child, you should start planning for it as soon as you know you're pregnant. Many kinds of day care are available, including one-on-one care out of the home or in it, group settings, and employer-sponsored facilities; the costs of these vary dramatically.

If you are not planning to use your local public school, you should also investigate the types and costs of private education. Educating a child from prekindergarten through high school graduation in a private school can easily cost more than four years of college. You have eighteen years to put aside the money for college, but the cost of day care, preschool care, or private primary school will be upon you very quickly; planning ahead can help ease the pain.

Housing. Your housing needs may change significantly with the birth of a child. You will probably need additional bedrooms and bathrooms and possibly recreational areas within your home, which may mean renovating your home or buying a new home. You may also want a vacation or weekend home. The costs of meeting these wishes are very high and should be planned for as early as possible.

Your child should be assured first-rate medical care and insurance coverage. Perhaps such coverage is available through your employer or your spouse's. Read your policies carefully. You may conclude that the deductibles are too high or that predictable and important expenses, such as dental or orthodontic work or eyeglasses, are not adequately covered. If so, you may wish to purchase additional coverage.

If you are separated or divorced from your child's father, you face the additional burden of coping with possibly inadequate or unreliable child support, custody arrangements, and possible litigation. Try to see that court-ordered child support payments and contributions to medical care and education costs are made. Seek the assistance of an attorney when necessary.

10

PROFESSIONAL FINANCIAL ADVISERS

As your professional standing grows, along with your income, your assets, and perhaps your dependents and financial responsibilities, you have an increased need for professional advisers. Once you have substantial assets and a relatively complicated financial existence, you will have to choose among varying options for savings, investment, and tax management, and will probably require the services of professional advisers to help you select the best choices for you and your particular situation. They can provide you with specific suggestions about the most effective and least costly ways to handle your money and accomplish your personal goals.

You will need to choose your advisers carefully. You should always interview them personally to make sure you are comfortable both with them and with their approach. Discuss precisely what services they will provide and for what price. If you are dissatisfied for any reason, whether because of the quality of advice or because of a lack of personal attention, change advisers.

When looking for professional advisers, you may want to ask for recommendations from friends and colleagues. However, it is probably not wise to use professionals who recommend each other, because it is unrealistic to expect them to offer differing advice or point out problems in the work of a friend. Your interests may suffer in consequence.

Financial planners. Although financial planners are not licensed, the Institute of Certified Financial Planners in Denver, Colorado publishes a list of its members, organized by geographical region. To qualify for the institute's certification, applicants must meet certain standards, including a minimum experience requirement. This is not a guarantee of quality, but it offers some help.

There are basically two kinds of financial planners. The first sells a product or service, such as stocks, bonds, or insurance, as a main business and does financial planning on the side for clients who purchase those products or services. Such people can provide excellent advice, but the arrangement raises the possibility of conflict of interest on the planner's part. A stockbroker, for example, is not likely to tell you that investing in stocks is not a good move in your situation even if that is the truth. You would be wise to seek a certified financial planner who isn't selling anything and who is therefore free to make honest recommendations in your best interest.

Although you may benefit from the planner's long experience in providing money management advice, you should not expect a financial planner to set goals for you or to make you live by your established budget or progress along your projected career path. A financial planner can only understand what you say you want and when you say you want it and then recommend ways for you to achieve your goals. You still have to decide what your goals are and what you are willing to do to accomplish them.

For example, if you want to retire in twenty years with an annual income of $40,000, a financial planner can make suggestions about how to invest your existing assets, how much you should save from your current income, and how you could invest those savings in order to accomplish that goal. But you are the one who has to decide whether or not to follow the advice.

Stockbrokers. Whereas investment advisers seek to advise you on your overall short-range and long-range investment plans, stockbrokers, both full-fee and discount brokers, are available to handle stock and bond purchases and sales. Full-fee brokers generally do some advisory work, while discount brokers only execute orders.

Mutual fund managers, of course, work for you if you buy shares in a mutual fund. They are generally not available to you on an ongoing basis to discuss your investments, however.

If you use a stockbroker, you need to find one who will analyze and understand your investing objectives, both short-term and long-term. The stockbroker should then advise you on appropriate investments, when to buy and sell, and which investments suit your short- and long-range financial and investment plans.

Your accountant. Your accountant should assist you in formulating your personal financial plan for meeting both current needs and short- and long-term goals. He or she should also advise you on tax planning and tax preparation.

Your accountant should be able to provide guidance on all business matters that require you to sign a contract, make an investment, or take on partners or investors; review all bank documents; and review the final draft of your will.

The range of areas in which your accountant's advice is essential is wide. In any given year, your accountant might help you start up a new business, sell an existing business or your interest in one, negotiate a mortgage or refinance a loan, revise or add to your will, and help you time charitable contributions or medical deductions in order to achieve the most advantageous tax treatment.

For example, if you own a business, there are tax implications to any form of organization you use, whether a sole proprietorship or a full-fledged corporation. An accountant can help you decide which form is most suitable for you and your situation. If you are selling a business, an accountant can help you work out the most advantageous arrangement. If your income taxes involve anything more complicated than straight salary and the standard deduction, an accountant may be able to suggest ways to minimize your tax liability.

You should employ a licensed certified public accountant (CPA) to assist you with tax planning, tax form preparation, meeting IRS audit requirements, and setting up and keeping the books for your personal finances or your own business. CPAs provide a broader range of services than tax preparers who are not licensed and who are available only to prepare your tax returns.

If your income is over $50,000, it's especially important to use a CPA. At that income level, you pay a sizable sum in federal, state, and other taxes, and it is worth seeking out a CPA who can orchestrate how you handle your books, how you pay your expenses, and how you take your deductions to ensure that you take advantage of the large number of complex tax provisions available to you. If your income is significantly smaller than $50,000, professional tax planning may well cost more than you are likely to save. In general, the higher your income, the more professional help you should seek to reduce your risk of losing a significant amount of money through sheer carelessness, poor planning, or ignorance of tax-saving provisions.

11

TAX PLANNING

Whatever your age and your financial status, you should always keep good tax records. Ideally, tax preparation and tax planning should be a monthly function; those who try to deal with tax concerns in early April, just before the IRS April 15 due date, are at a major disadvantage. First, many tax deductions can be taken only if you have proper records to support your claims; these include unreimbursed business expenses, medical expenses, and expenses for the care and support of dependents.

You should also watch things closely enough so that you can plan for the next tax year as well as the current one. There are many ways to handle income and expenses; being able to take advantage of every possible tax break requires careful planning and execution.

You may find it worthwhile to get a copy of one of the many annual tax guides available and review it with your accountant to determine which areas you need to watch most closely. Tax planning allows you to purchase and sell assets at the most favorable time, take maximum deductions, and pay necessary expenses in the best way at the best time.

Careful planning can, for instance, avoid the alternative minimum tax (AMT) imposed on high-income individuals who face no tax liability because high deductions leave them with no taxable income. The timing of the sale of stocks, bonds, investment real estate, art, and collectibles can determine whether or not you will face the ATM since you are required to pay capital gains tax to reflect your loss in the year in which it occurred. Deferring a deduction can leave you with enough income to avoid the ATM and instead pay the lower regular income tax.

Medical expenses and unreimbursed business expenses are other areas where planning is required. Because each has a deductible, grouping two years' expenses into one year may enable you to claim the deduction, whereas splitting the expenses over two years may mean not qualifying for the deduction in both years.

It is to your distinct advantage to keep thorough and accurate records of all business expenses for which you are not reimbursed. You should list the following:

- Expense item description
- Date of expense
- Business purpose
- Name of business client or associate
- Method of payment
- Invoice or receipt

12

SETTING CAREER GOALS

It is essential that you assess your current career status and think about where you would like your career to take you in one year, three years, five years, even twenty years. Different people have different career goals; you need to be honest with yourself about what you really want and then determine whether your current path is likely to get you there.

For example, if it is your goal to work part-time for income and satisfaction and to be available for travel with your family or to care for dependents, it is important that you select a career that does not dominate your personal life and does not require late hours, irregular hours, or business travel.

Selling real estate, for example, often appeals to women because it can be done part time and has flexible hours. However, to sell real estate successfully, you are apt to have to work evenings and weekends, which is the time people are free to go looking at houses. If your goal is to be at home when the children are out of school, this is not likely to be a successful arrangement. On the other hand, if your husband works a nine-to-five job and your goal is to have someone at home all the time, this could be the perfect arrangement.

Remember that what you are looking for is an arrangement that works for you personally, not something that is the ideal for someone in an entirely different situation. Remember also that once you set up limitations, for whatever reason, the highest-paying jobs and the positions with the greatest responsibility and opportunity for advancement are unlikely to be open to you.

If, on the other hand, your short-term goal, covering perhaps three to five years, is a part-time position but you look forward to full-time responsible work with some business travel further down the line, you should discuss this matter with the personnel or human resources department of your company. Many companies will work with you to plot a long-range plan that permits you to limit your responsibilities for several years and to undertake a larger commitment to the corporation at a later date. If you are a key employee who is developing significant skills, it is important to both you and the company that you not be put in dead-end positions that offer no challenge. You might even manage to work out an agreement that lets you do some work at home and perhaps seek additional education to increase your skills during your part-time phase.

13

CAREER COUNSELING

Your search for career counseling should start at your university, whether you are just completing a degree or have been out of school for many years. Career counseling and placement services are frequently combined at university offices, but in fact they are two entirely separate functions. Career counseling seeks to determine what you want to do, what you're good at, what you're bad at, and where you might fit in in the business world, academia, or even the military. Although many university career counseling departments may seem geared to people just starting out, they can be equally valuable for older graduates, especially those contemplating a change in career.

Take advantage of all services offered. You should probably start with a battery of aptitude tests. These tests are very broad and will not tell you exactly what career you should pursue, but they can call to your attention a wide group of areas in which you might do well and warn you against at least one or two areas for which you are probably unsuited.

The career counseling office should also offer assistance in preparing a proper résumé or résumés. Every type of job or position for which you are going to apply really should have a customized résumé that reflects your ability to meet the needs of the company. General résumés that simply list education and work experience are not as effective.

Your career counselor should also be able to give you up-to-date information about which corporations, government groups, and academic groups are hiring and where the growth is and where cutbacks are under way.

The career counseling office will be able to project a likely salary and promotion scenario in specific industries for someone with your background and credentials. Again, this will be general but should give you some guidance. For instance, investment banking pays huge salaries and bonuses, and academia pays low salaries and no bonuses. On the other hand, investment banking is currently very hard hit by the recession, and job losses are severe and mounting. Certain areas of academia, such as chemical and electrical engineering, are currently facing a shortage of qualified candidates, and job security in these areas looks good.

Review your plans for seeking advanced degrees with your career counselor. Ten years ago, an MBA from one of the top business schools seemed to assure a high-paid entry level position, excellent job security, and a future of high earnings. Currently, there is some question about the value of an MBA when the cost of acquiring the degree is measured against the immediate salary advantage. It is possible in this economy that it is better to plan on getting an MBA after you are working full time, especially if your employer will provide some financial assistance.

Finally, career counseling offices at universities should be able to provide some input regarding regional economies and the health of major industries located in those regions. For instance, in the late '80s there was a real estate bust in Texas, and prospects for pursuing a career there in any related industry were not good. In the early '90s, fortunes have reversed somewhat. Currently, the Pacific Northwest is considered "hot." There has been a major population shift to that area, opening up not just job opportunities in established industries, such as fishing, but a whole host of service industries required to support the new surge in population. Conversely, of course, areas losing large segments of their population do not represent desirable opportunities for employment.

Once you have exhausted the services available through the career counselor at your university, explore what's available in your trade organization (or union where applicable). These organizations may not have the funding to offer batteries of psychological tests, but they can be the source of the most up-to-date information regarding opportunities within a particular field. They also serve as job marts. Skilled counselors in trade organizations are particularly useful to young professionals not yet in a position to rely on their own network of contacts. Before networking was so popular, events at trade organizations provided pretty much the same opportunities.

Many large trade organizations even offer scholarships, training programs, and awards for achievement in their efforts at continued education within their field. Again, it only makes sense to take advantage of everything available. The most important thing to you in planning and orchestrating your career is knowledge.

Career counselors in trade organizations may even be willing to arrange appointments for you with industry leaders. While such interviews and conversations may not necessarily lead immediately to job openings, these are very useful contacts to have and such interviews give you an important opportunity to observe how things are done at the top. Occasionally such meetings can lead to a "mentoring" arrangement.

Corporate Career Counseling. All major corporations offer career counseling services. Remember, however, that the objective of the corporation in offering these services is to maximize your potential and contribution within that corporation. Some corporations offer access to psychological tests, access to senior executives, access to training programs, assistance in additional education.

Of particular interest are programs set up to develop female managers since the managerial ranks in almost all cases are still heavily male. Again, it only makes sense to take advantage of everything. It will be your decision whether you wish to stay with a particular corporation or even within a particular field of interest, but it certainly makes sense to explore fully your potential contribution and options with your current employer.

Universities and government agencies offer a somewhat limited version of the same kind of program.

Outside professional organizations. Through word of mouth or even through a review of your yellow pages, you can find innumerable career counseling operations in any major city. These services will all be for fee only. You may be required to pay an upfront fee of several hundred dollars to cover psychological testing, interviews, and résumé development, or you may pay by the hour to speak with a counselor or to use the service's resources and files and research library.

These professional counselors are generally the first choice of people who feel they are at a dead-end at their corporation or in their field or geographical location. In many such cases, adequate facilities are not available at an alma mater or through a trade organization. Because of the importance of guiding your own career and controlling its direction yourself, it is important to seek out these professional counselors if the resources discussed earlier are not available to you.

14

KEEPING VISIBLE

Whether you're working part-time or full-time or planning your own business, make a point of remaining visible in your field. Join trade organizations, attend seminars, and subscribe to trade publications. In many professions, trade publications are by far the best source of industry and personnel gossip. You need to stay on top of such gossip so that you can spot opportunities and move on them quickly. If you learn of important developments months after they occur, someone else may already have taken advantage of the unexpected opportunities that arise constantly.

Most career advancement in most professions is the result of personal referrals and references. If you are visible in your field, perhaps on radio and TV and in appropriate publications, you will be on people's minds. When there is an interesting opening, these people will think of you.

Your ability to reciprocate by steering business to colleagues will be greatly enhanced if you see and interact with other professionals in your field on a regular basis at various professional functions.

Writing and Speaking to Colleagues in Your Field. It is important to take advantage of every opportunity offered you to write for trade magazines and related publications in your field or for your local newspaper. It also makes sense to take advantage of speaking opportunities when they arise. Whether you are just starting out, peaking, or preparing for a move, it's good for your name to be seen in print and your face to be seen in public in ways that associate you importantly with your field. You should accept these opportunities even if you have to seek professional help in preparing your article or speech.

If you have not been offered any opportunity to speak in your field, volunteer. There are often speaking slots open at conventions, trade shows, and honorary dinners. These slots are hard to fill unless the sponsor is offering a fee. Since your objective is exposure rather than an honorarium, you're likely to find that your offer to speak is quickly accepted.

15

GROWTH POTENTIAL

Step back periodically and analyze the growth potential of your field and your particular position in that field in terms of national and international trends. Certain fields and businesses are shrinking, while others are expanding; it is always best to be part of a field that shows both short-term and long-term growth potential. As the population ages, for example, industries serving older people are likely to thrive. The older population needs health care, housing, and leisure activities, as well as goods and services geared to their needs and abilities.

The effects of a shrinking market are illustrated by the changing prospects of real estate professionals. During the 1980s, there was an unprecedented real estate boom in the United States. Real estate brokerage operations that had employed two or three part-time brokers expanded in many cases to forty or fifty brokers. When the bubble burst in the late 1980s and early 1990s, however, large numbers of brokers were laid off, with little hope of ever regaining their former positions or earning the kinds of salaries and commissions they had made during the early 1980s.

At the same time, the United States is experiencing a desperate shortage of health care workers. Health organizations are willing to assist financially in the training of new employees. There are openings at all levels, from entry-level positions requiring no college education through executive positions that in some cases require MBAs. People laid off in industries such as real estate might do well to consider moving to an industry such as health care, which is growing rapidly now and will certainly continue to do so for the next several decades as the population ages.

Fields Open to Older Workers. Professionals, lawyers, doctors, and accountants, who tend to operate on their own, have always worked until they chose to retire. Some fields, such as advertising, however, have long been notorious as "a young person's industry." Movies and books have often portrayed advertising executives as feeling over the hill and useless by the time they reach their early forties. Although this is strictly a matter of image manipulation, it can be devastating to have to leave your field in mid-career.

The solution to finding yourself displaced or unwanted while you are still relatively young is to switch into a field that is growing and that appreciates the skills of a working veteran. Such opportunities were abundant in the early 1990s in teaching, health care, and international product marketing. If you're considering such a move, you should restructure your résumé to emphasize broad skills that apply to the new industry. At the same time you may need to obtain additional training and education in the field of your choice. Frequently your new employer will cover all or some of this expense.

The Glass Ceiling. In addition to facing the same threats to status, stability, and comfort that a professional man faces, women must also deal with the problem of the "glass ceiling." This phrase refers to the perceived notion in some corporations and professions that there is a certain level beyond which women cannot, as a rule, advance. There are exceptions who make it through all the way to the top, but they are very few and far between. Women's reactions to the glass ceiling tend to vary by age. Younger women refuse to recognize its existence and simply steam ahead. Women in their thirties and forties know that it exists in certain circumstances and try to plan a path around it, if not a direct assault. Large numbers of women start their own businesses at the point in their careers where they encounter this obstacle. Older women in the work force tend to take it for granted.

The glass ceiling was and is a very real thing for older women. Middle-aged women are beginning to break through it, and it is unlikely to be a major factor in the careers of young women just now entering the work force.

16

INVESTING IN YOUR CAREER

As a rule, any investment in your education is worthwhile. A college degree is probably desirable for success for your profession, and a graduate degree may soon be necessary as well. Education, however, does not have a beginning and an end. Whatever your profession, you should stay on top of it by attending seminars, reading trade publications, taking an occasional course in new concepts, and staying in touch with the opinionmakers in your profession.

If you find yourself in a low-growth or no-growth profession, you must face the question of whether to make a switch in mid-career. This can be a daunting prospect, but keep in mind that much of what you have learned in the business world is transferable to another field. However, you may need additional formal training in your new area. For instance, if you switch into the health care field, you may require additional education. On the other hand, if you have experience managing a large group of people, dealing with administrative matters, and working with a significant budget, these skills are readily transferable to a high-level position in your new field.

Stay Technologically Up to Date. We live in a society ruled by technology, and this fact is not likely to change in the foreseeable future. No matter what skills you may have in your particular field, it is worthwhile for you to learn to understand and master the technical end of things.

Analysts in the United States are already predicting that there will be a shortage of technical workers in upcoming decades. This shortage opens a wonderful opportunity for people in the second phases of their careers—if they take the time now to seek the proper training and education.

All universities, for example, currently offer courses in computer literacy, which is fast becoming a requirement in many fields. Another skill much in demand is foreign language facility; courses are offered in all major metropolitan areas as well as at universities in the languages most needed by those involved in international commerce.

Relocating. A career move into a growth area might also entail a relocation. If you are entering the field of computer software design, for instance, you might find it desirable to move to the Boston or San Francisco area. A relocation can be expensive and psychologically disruptive for you and your household, and such a move needs to be weighed carefully. Professional men have long faced the prospect of several relocations during their careers; professional women now face exactly the same prospect.

Your employer may offer relocation assistance if you or your spouse is transferred to a new region of the country. Willingness to accept a transfer can be important if you hope to gain experience in several areas of your field; financial help from your employer in meeting the expense of moving, selling your house, and finding employment for your spouse in the new location can make relocation less difficult.

Although it's a common belief that the "action" is at the main office, in reality many reputations are made "in the field." Tackling and succeeding at the management of a distant branch office, for example, can lead to a big promotion when you return to the home office.

Women have traditionally been unwilling to accept relocation because it disrupted the lives of their children and husband. To reduce the trauma, more and more corporations are assisting the entire family as it makes the move.

36

17

EVALUATING EMPLOYMENT OPPORTUNITIES

On the surface, it's easy to see that if one job pays $30,000 and another pays $40,000, the one offering a higher salary has an obvious advantage. On the other hand, the situation may be more complicated than that. Early in your career, and even in mid-career, you may be better off taking a position that pays a little less but is closer to the center of power than one that pays a little more but is further from the real power in the company. The best way to learn is to work for the decision-maker. If you learn fast and become valuable to your employer, and if you also have the experience of seeing first-hand how things are run, you will progress more quickly than if you start with a higher salary but get no exposure to the decision-making process and bottom-line responsibility.

It can also pay off if you're willing to accept a position, perhaps for a fixed period of time, in which you receive in-depth training in an area you know you'll need later. Again, in such a situation, salary is not the first consideration. If, for instance, you have an opportunity to receive intensive sales training, it's probably worth taking a low salary temporarily to have the benefit of this valuable experience.

Weighing Salary and Benefits. If you are working on a straight salary basis, it is relatively easy to figure out how much you make and how much you are likely to make in the same job and company over the next few years. If you receive both salary and commission, your income becomes somewhat more difficult to predict. You will have to monitor industrywide trends and work out projections for your company based on the best information available in trade magazines and through trade organizations.

Do not neglect to add in the value of employee benefits. You probably receive some health insurance through your employer, and you may have life insurance as well.

The value of these benefits can easily be established by checking the cost of paying for these items privately. Call one or two insurance companies, for instance, and price their life and health insurance policies. Follow the same procedure with tuition payment plans, child care allowances, or any other benefits you take advantage of.

Companies offer a grab bag of other benefits to their employees. Your company may offer attractive educational benefits, for example. A recent development has been the provision of assistance in obtaining dependent care. This assistance takes many forms. You may be able to take off several hours a week to care for children or aging parents. Your company may have an on-site day care center for preschool children, which is available to you at little or no cost, or it may offer vouchers to be used at the day care center of your choosing. A more recent innovation is the provision of assistance in caring for aging and dependent parents, again in the form of on-site or off-site day care or vouchers you may use at the program of your choice.

Remember that the value of any benefit depends on your situation. Education or child care benefits you will never use are of no value to you, so don't include them in your calculations.

BENEFITS YOU FORFEIT WHEN YOU LEAVE YOUR JOB (AND THE COST OF REPLACEMENT)

Item	Your Cost to Replace
Health insurance	$1,000–$3,500 per year
Life insurance	$250–$2,000
Disability insurance	$1500–$3,000
Pension/corporate profit-sharing and 401-k plans	Not replaceable
Travel and entertainment	Amount allotted
Corporate car (self-driven)	Car lease, $200–$500 monthly
	Car insurance, $1,000 per year
	Garage, $100–$500 a month
	Maintenance, $500 annually
Telephone, mail room, photocopying service	$100+ per month
Dependent care allowance	Amount allotted, usually $400–$1,200 a year
Corporate car service	$100 per month+
Tuition assistance	Amount allotted

18

YOUR RÉSUMÉ

Always keep an up-to-date résumé handy; you never can tell when you might be asked for one. On the other hand, if you are seriously pursuing a particular position, you should always prepare a customized résumé geared specifically to that position. If you are simultaneously pursuing two different positions, you should prepare résumés that highlight abilities and achievements applicable to each of them.

Even if you are happily employed, I believe you should always take advantage of interviews sought by prospective employers even if you have no intention of pursuing the career path involved. Periodically getting feedback on your qualifications and current position in your field can be an educational experience. You can find out not only which of your talents and abilities are highly valued but also where you fall short.

However, interviewing can get sticky if the call comes from a competitor. In this case, you may decide not to accept the interview out of loyalty to your current employer.

Preparing a Résumé if You Have Never Worked for a Salary. All women work, but many do not collect a salary. Homemakers manage their households, raise their children, and assist their husbands in business and social matters. Many of these homemakers also work extensively in charitable organizations and in their children's schools.

If you have never worked for a salary, your résumé should focus on three things: marketable skills, such as writing skills; unpaid supervisory experience, including the number of people supervised (a volunteer director of a major charity may have supervised as many as one or two dozen paid employees); and the size of the budget managed. You have managed your home budget, of course, but an employer is likely to be more interested in the budget you handled at your charity, at your child's school, or at your college.

Employers are looking for marketable skills, management experience, bottom-line budget experience, and longevity at one activity. Emphasize all of these points in your résumé.

19

HEADHUNTERS AND EMPLOYMENT AGENCIES

One of the ironies of dealing with headhunters (executive placement organizations) is that their policy is: "Don't call us, we'll call you." All of the major executive recruiters maintain enormous computer files of executives in all types of businesses in the United States and abroad, generally from upper-middle management or the lower vice-presidential level up to top management.

Because headhunters work for corporate clients, not potential employees, sending off résumés to one generally does not accomplish much. Headhunters build their data banks through personal contacts, personal references, trade publications, and activities of trade organizations.

If you are contacted by a headhunter, your file can be deemed "active," and your name will surface periodically as a potential candidate for a number of positions. Getting into the file is the hard part. To accomplish this, you must be visible in your field.

Employment agencies, on the other hand, operate in just the reverse fashion. While requests come in to them from corporations, they technically work for the job applicant and collect a fee for their service (which is usually paid by the employer). You should be familiar with the major employment agencies in your given field; it does not hurt to periodically send them information about your activities. An occasional meeting or lunch with the key players is probably also a good idea, simply to keep your options open.

Finally, there are outplacement agencies, which assist victims of downsizing or other corporate cuts. Those referred to outplacement agencies have generally been let go through no fault of their own. Frequently the former employer pays for outplacement services for long-time or particularly senior employees. Outplacement agencies work with executive recruiters and employment agencies as well as heads of corporate personnel departments.

20

WORKING AT HOME

A recent *New York Times* headline read, "Fleeing the Office and Its Distractions: Almost Half of the Executives Who Work At Home Are Men, and Most Are Managers."

Working at home is a mixed blessing. On the positive side, it is clearly convenient; there's no commute, no dressing for the office, no office interruptions and distractions. If you are disciplined, it is also possible to get a lot more done. On the negative side, household disruptions can be as bad as office disruptions; if you are going to work seriously at home, you need to set aside a serious office space and demand quiet. In addition, many people who work at home work themselves too hard. There is no nine-to-five structure, so home workers frequently start early in the morning and even more frequently work after dinner and occasionally late into the night. While this produces a lot of work, it can also lead to burnout and isolation.

There used to be a presumption that if you worked at home, either you couldn't get an office job or you were working part-time. As *The New York Times* headline indicates, that is no longer the case. In fact, many senior managers are demanding to work at home, as a sort of perk. They apparently produce as much or more work than they did in the office while avoiding a tiring and time-consuming commute as well as distractions from day-to-day minor matters.

If your day at home consists of working on your computer, on your phone, and on your fax, you will probably not encounter any zoning or licensing problems. If, on the other hand, you accept deliveries, make noise, or work with other employees, you may run into licensing, zoning, and even co-op board restrictions. It's best to check out whether you're likely to run into these difficulties before you go to the trouble and expense of setting up your home office. For instance, in a residential apartment building, whether a cooperative or a condominium, there are probably rules against having employees work in your apartment, having commercial mail delivered, having messengers make deliveries, and using any kind of commercial machine that makes a lot of noise. Furthermore, group activities that might pose a noise or health threat are certain to be prohibited.

In single-family housing in residential communities, things are less well-defined. If your home is in a residentially-zoned area, you will not be able to post any kind of commercial sign, convert outbuildings to commercial use, serve food for profit, install employees and their automobiles, or overuse existing water supplies and trash removal services.

Regardless of your housing set-up, it's prudent to consider possible roadblocks to working at home before you go too far in getting your business in gear.

21

YOUR CAREER SHOULD PROVIDE WHAT YOU NEED WHEN YOU NEED IT

The critical thing to remember is that your career and income function in one way when you're starting out, another when you are married, perhaps with children, another when you are divorced or widowed or simply choose to live alone, and yet another when you have aging parents. These phases may, of course, overlap. Your career, the satisfaction it brings you, the time it takes, and the income it earns all need to match your life phase.

For instance, when you are starting out, you may have a great deal of personal freedom and no dependents. Perhaps travel and meeting new people are high on your list of priorities.

Once married, you may wish to reduce or eliminate business travel; once children arrive, scheduling your day around them becomes your top priority. Business travel becomes extremely difficult. You may even wish to work part-time or at home during this time. While your goal prior to the birth of your children may have been to advance as rapidly as possible through as many promotions and salary increases as possible, after the birth of your children you may prefer a stable situation in which promotions and salary increases are not a priority—coping may be your main priority.

Once your children are older, you may wish to resume your business travel, increase your responsibilities, and get additional professional training. If you are widowed or divorced at some point, you may again wish to build up the social aspect of your job in an effort to get out more and meet people.

Finally, if you find yourself responsible for an aging parent, you may return to a mode similar to that of the new mother, in which stability, possibly through part-time work, is uppermost.

22

LEAVING CORPORATE LIFE FOR A BUSINESS START-UP

While corporate life can at times be frustrating, bureaucratic, stressful, boring, and dead-end, you should never lose sight of the fact that in many cases it provides a certain stability, a fixed and regular paycheck, and important benefits such as health insurance, life insurance, disability insurance, profit-sharing plans, pension plans, company cars, travel and entertainment allowances, and corporate discounts.

Business start-ups, despite their strong appeal, rarely offer the same safety, stability, predictability, income, or benefits. On the other hand, they do offer enormous psychological benefits. These include freedom to innovate, control over all aspects of the business, flexible hours, the choice of location, control over staff selection, bottom-line responsibility, and freedom to set short-range and long-range goals. You may also enjoy tax benefits, real-estate opportunities, and professional recognition.

Self-employment or small business start-ups can be full-time or part-time and can be undertaken at the peak of your career or when you retire from another occupation. They can be done alone or with partners, with no outside financing or with partial or total outside financing.

The decision to leave a corporate environment and start your own business has an impact on you and your family and dependents. It changes, many times irreversibly, your standard of living and your relationship with your children, your spouse or companion, and perhaps even your parents.

The success of any start-up ultimately depends on the viability of your product or service. Can you produce it in such a way that you can make a profit large enough to fund your business and pay your living expenses? Can you do this in a reasonable number of hours? Does your product or service have growth potential and is it likely to support you for the long term, including your retirement years?

It is not uncommon for those who leave the corporate world to start a business to experience a drastic drop in their living standard. The change frequently seems worth it when the trade-offs are considered. It is not worth it if the new venture does not provide some long-term possibility of funding your living expenses, long-range financial goals, dependent responsibilities, and retirement and health care needs.

Budding entrepreneurs are everywhere. You see them in high school, in college, in small towns, in big cities, and, increasingly, in retirement communities and among those who have been retired early, downsized, and eliminated.

One important economic trend favoring the entrepreneur is the tendency among corporations to eliminate full-time jobs in favor of part-time jobs and freelance assignments.

If you are contemplating starting a business of your own, be sure to discuss it with your accountant, your lawyer, and possibly your banker and your insurance agent. They can save you from costly mistakes.

Corporate Preparation for Your Own Business. If your long-term goal is to open your own business, you should plan carefully how you are going to extract from your corporate employment as much useful experience as possible. At the bare minimum, you need to have experience in sales, experience hiring and managing a diverse group of people, experience with a budget, and, preferably, responsibility for the bottom line (at least on a department-head level).

If you need to be familiar with a variety of national markets, use the opportunity for business travel at your corporation to gain that familiarity. Study all the information available at your corporation regarding the competition; learn how marketing plans are formulated, how sales projections are put together, and how paid advertising, sales promotion, and publicity are used.

Finally, take advantage of *any* opportunity for higher education in your field that is paid for by your employer.

23

ONE COMPANY, "CRADLE TO GRAVE"

One company, now and forever? Don't bank on it. There was a time when people went to work for the ABC Company and could expect to get regular promotions, regular raises, and generous employer benefits if they performed well. Now you have to expect the unexpected. The American economy is no longer growing on all fronts. Some industries are growing and present excellent opportunities, but others are constricting or disappearing. American workers have learned what it's like to be downsized, laid off, and retired early; they've also seen their companies go through mergers and bankruptcies. It's best to hedge your bets and be prepared to cover by yourself necessities that were previously provided by an employer. For instance, if you're laid off you may find it necessary to take out your own health insurance. You may be able to extend or adapt your former corporate policy or you may decide to try one of the newer alternatives such as health maintenance organizations (HMO), preferred-provider organizations, or some variation on these (see Key 29). Another benefit you may well miss is funds for education. It has become increasingly difficult for corporations to keep such programs while streamlining. Again, it's best to lay your own plans. For instance, you can enroll in an MBA program that offers classes in the evening over several years. The financial and time strain on yourself can thus be kept to a minimum.

Loss of Your Professional Status. Much has been written about the trauma men face when they are fired, retired, demoted, or left unexpectedly afloat. The same problems occur for women, and their reaction is the same. The loss of status, office services, travel and entertainment expense account, professional memberships, office camaraderie, and involvement in a life's work are devastating to deal with. Finding yourself unemployed is deeply depressing and frightening; having your position declared irrelevant or eliminated is threatening and puzzling; and being stripped of your professional standing and perks is irritating, inconvenient, and a real challenge to your self-esteem.

A support structure that includes outplacement companies, a network of professional acquaintances, university services, and of course comforting friends and family somehow get you through it and back on your feet. Still, recovery is not quick, and a certain leeriness, cynicism, and bitterness can linger.

A woman who has lost her position goes through several stages, generally starting with shock and disbelief. They are quickly followed by depression, feelings of worthlessness, and grave doubts about the importance of one's work, one's professional life, and one's future. This stage is inevitably followed by anger, even rage. It is generally at this stage that the woman takes action. She has to reassess where she lives, how she lives, her finances, her personal life, and the potential of her chosen professional field.

It is frustrating, irritating, and exhausting to start again. However, for those who do, the benefits can be substantial. They may have been dead-ended for longer than they were willing to realize, and a shock like this can jolt them into taking a new direction, one that they would have wanted sooner or later.

Going through the entire process may take only a few weeks or a month in some women, but it can drag out for more than a year in others. For those who do not come out of the cycle and begin responding, professional help can be a good idea. A therapist can be useful helping sort out priorities, set goals, and overcome crises.

24

THE COMPUTER CONSULTANT

If you are past the third decade of your life, the chances are excellent that you are not computer literate. Your school-age child may be more savvy about computers than you are—in fact, your preschooler may be, because they have probably had more exposure to them. Children are comfortable with them, and they know how to use them for fun or education. Many adults do not.

Even if you have already recognized the obvious advantage of computerizing many or most phases of your business, you may still resist computerizing your non-professional needs—legal, insurance, medical, household management, and health papers. You can easily store all pertinent information related to these areas, as well as options available to you, in your personal computer. If you do not have a home computer for your personal and professional needs, hire a computer consultant who will analyze your records and ongoing activities in your professional area and recommend several computers and software for your consideration. The counsellor should then familiarize you with the workings of the computer and help you become computer literate.

Your counsellor should also discuss with you the pros and cons of buying or leasing a computer and advise you on whether you require the services of a programmer to handle your personal and professional needs at home. You can usually find listings of computer consultants through your local computer store, through the yellow pages, or even through your local university. Costs start at about $50 per hour.

25

YOUR LAWYER

Your lawyer should advise you on and review any situation with potential legal ramifications. This includes not only lawsuits or legal conflicts like divorce proceedings or custody arrangements but also any financial arrangements that involve legal papers like leases, mortgages, and loans.

A lawyer should also advise you on major investments like residential or commercial real estate (Key 26). There are innumerable details involved in such a purchase, from a title search to responsibility for back taxes, that can involve you in unexpected—and unnecessary—expenses if not handled properly. You need a lawyer to watch out for your interests. Never simply allow the lawyer for the other party to handle the entire deal. What you save in legal fees at the time could cost you later on.

One woman bought a house and let the seller's attorney, recommended by the real estate broker, handle everything. As a result, she didn't find out until the house was hers that it was in a flood area and uninsurable. Her subsequent costs were hundreds of times higher than those she would have incurred had she retained her own lawyer in the first place.

If you have any assets or dependents, you should have a will. There is no other way to ensure that your assets are distributed as you intend and that your dependents are cared for as you wish. Your lawyer will keep a copy of your will in addition to the copy you keep.

Checklist for preparation of your will. Wills should include the following:

• Your name
• Current primary residence address

- Telephone number
- Address and telephone number of your second home, where applicable, and your business
- Any unlisted phone numbers in your name
- Information about your executor or coexecutors: name, address, phone number, business address, and phone number; relation to you
- Identification of executor or coexecutors as relatives or business or personal associates
- Where appropriate, a guardian for your child or children
- Guardian's name, address (business and residence), telephone number (business and residence), relation to you
- Exactly what you want the guardian to do, unless you have covered this elsewhere in a separate trust. It is standard to include instructions regarding: education, religion, disposal of assets, living arrangements, and social arrangements. This issue can get quite complicated if there has been a divorce or separation or if you have responsibility currently for children who are not your own, such as stepchildren.
- Instructions regarding payment of all of your current debts. Only after your debts are paid can your executor properly distribute the assets of your estate.
- Funeral arrangements that you desire. Unpleasant as this is to contemplate, you are actually helping your executor to handle a delicate matter. Being specific will probably prevent disagreements among spouse, children, parents, friends.
- If you prefer cremation to burial or wish to donate specific organs to a hospital or organ bank, you must so stipulate. Do not think that because you have mentioned your preferences to your lawyer or oldest child or minister, your wishes will be carried out upon your death. Family members may insist you hadn't really meant it and impose their own personal wishes at this sensitive time.

- All trusts you have established. You may have trusts for maintenance or sale of your business, financial arrangements regarding your children, or charitable donations to specific organizations.
- For each trust, detailed information about the trustees you have chosen. These may well be different from your executor or executors.
- Make sure that your will is properly witnessed.
- List all beneficiaries. Be very specific regarding full name, address, phone number, business address, and relation to you. Also specify the assets assigned to each beneficiary.

It is helpful to include with your will a current listing of all of your assets, including their whereabouts.

26

REAL ESTATE

Real estate is a major investment, a major commitment, a major factor in your quality of life. It must be a priority.

Owning a home has a powerful emotional component. In addition, until recently, home ownership was viewed as a safe investment. It seemed that the price of real estate always went up. This is no longer necessarily the case. The large number of baby boomers who bought houses will be trying to sell them in coming years, but they are likely to find fewer buyers for them. As a result, prices will stay level or even drop. When you combine stable prices with the effect of inflation, owning a home, especially if you are unfortunate enough to be in an economically depressed area, could be the wrong choice financially.

You also need to consider the size of your house. Needs in this area change as you move through life. If you are near retirement and your children are grown, or if you are living alone, a ten-room house may be much less appealing than it was when you had young children at home. Perhaps it is time to have a smaller house with newer amenities and no maintenance or mortgage worries.

As this book is being written, homeowners are experiencing the terribly painful realization that their house may not be, at least in the short term, a sure-fire investment. In many parts of the country, real estate prices have dropped as much as 30 percent from their highs in the 1980s. Homeowners with mortgages and home equity loans equal to *more* than their current equity in their properties are in a grim situation; many could not cover their debt if they sold their houses. How long will this situation go on? No one knows, but there are sure to be regional differences; some areas of the country will experience an upswing in prices while others, particularly those that experienced the greatest price inflation in the past years, will crash.

There are many attractive rental opportunities at this time, especially in areas that experienced overbuilding of one- and two-bedroom condominiums. In any scenario comparing renting and buying, however, you should remember that in order to get a rental benefit, you must invest the money you would have used for the down payment and mortgage payments on an owned apartment or home at a rate greater than the rate at which real estate is appreciating.

For example, if you have $30,000 available and you are trying to decide whether to rent or buy, you can try to calculate what the value of a house priced at $150,000, which you could buy with your $30,000 down payment, might be in ten years. However, this is risky in the current economy. If you had done this in 1980, your house might have doubled or even tripled in value by 1990. If you did such a calculation in 1990, you might have concluded that the same house will essentially hold its value for the next ten years; worse, it may lose value.

On the other hand, investing the $30,000 right now at perhaps 8 percent while at the same time renting and building no equity might be an appealing prospect. Of course, your investment, if not insured, could fail.

There is unfortunately no easy way to decide whether to buy or rent. Your decision will be influenced not only by the current state of the economy but by your housing needs now and in the future. Unpredictable events, such as divorce, job loss, or health problems, will have a great impact and may cause you to change your decision down the road.

Housing expenses

Owning	Renting
mortgage	rent
property taxes	utilities
insurance	
maintenance (indoors and outdoors)	
major renovations and repairs	
utilities	
heat	

Owning a home. Mortgage payments, property taxes, and heat may well add up to less than rent payments. Maintenance costs are variable, depending on the state of the property to begin with and the extent of any outdoor property. In a coop or condominium, there is a monthly maintenance payment that generally includes property taxes. Major repairs should be anticipated and planned for. For example, a roof will need to be replaced every fifteen to twenty-five years. You should anticipate this, and put aside money for such repairs ahead of time to avoid unpleasant surprises. Bear in mind also the fact that although your mortgage payments will remain stable, all other costs will rise along with inflation.

Renting a home. The rent on the equivalent amount of space will probably cost more than the necessary costs of owning a home. (After all, the landlord intends to make a profit.) In addition, you must expect your rent to go up every time your lease is renewed. It is possible that in a weak real estate market your rent may not increase, but don't bank on it.

Should you buy or should you rent? This section contains a checklist of the advantages of renting and buying real estate. In addition to these items, you of course need to factor in your personal circumstances and the state of the economy and real estate market in your locale.

Advantages of renting:
• Renting allows you greater personal flexibility. You are free to leave at the end of your lease.

- You incur no debt
- You incur minimal out-of-pocket expenses when moving in—security deposit, broker's fee, possibly minor cosmetic construction and decorating.
- There is no danger of losing equity value since you don't own the unit.
- Upkeep and maintenance, including major items such as plumbing, are the landlord's problem, not yours.
- A rental is not likely to affect employment decisions such as whether to relocate, because you do not stand to lose much. If your prospective employer is willing to absorb certain real estate losses, such as the unexpired part of your lease, you are in a better position if you are renting and the commitment is therefore minimal than if you own your home and therefore have a major commitment.
- You can invest the sum you would have used for a down payment and build capital that way.

Advantages of owning:
- The major advantage of owning may be psychological. It fosters a feeling of security, stability, and community.
- You have an immediate equity position in a major investment.
- Since mortgage payments must be made monthly, you are forced to continue to invest in a major asset.
- Home ownership has important tax advantages, including deductibility of the interest on your mortgage.
- Equity in a home generally provides security for loans you may wish to take.
- Your home may become the location of a business start-up.
- Sale of residential real estate may later fund your children's education, your retirement, or care for aging parents or spouse.

How much can you afford for monthly mortgage payments? The rule of thumb banks use in figuring what mortgage you may qualify for is that your monthly mortgage payment should not exceed 25 to 30 percent of your gross take-home pay. Most Americans exceed this rather dramatically, spending closer to 50 percent. Such high payments are difficult to manage over the long term and generally lead to late payment or default on other items.

Most home purchases require a 20 percent down payment. Banks may be flexible on this matter during upswings in economic cycles and may accept as little as 10 percent; in bad times they may ask for as much as 30 percent. Cooperatives generally require a 50 percent down payment; some of the most exclusive buildings require 75 percent or even 100 percent. Condominiums are financed along terms similar to those available for houses.

Both fixed-rate and adjustable-rate mortgages are available, and it's a judgment call as to which is better. Fixed-rate mortgages are preferable if interest rates are likely to rise; adjustable rates are better if interest rates are coming down. Unfortunately, no one seems to be able to predict with accuracy what interest rates will do.

27

TYPES OF HOUSING

If you are just out of college or graduate school or just out of a marriage that didn't work out, you might be interested in starter housing—that is, a house that serves your current needs but in which you do not plan to stay forever. Probably, a rental will best suit your needs; it requires only an investment of one or two months' security, a commitment for one, two, or three years on a lease, and an obligation to pay utilities. It's easy to get into and out of with very little stress and strain. However, when your lease expires, whether it's after one year or fifteen years in the rental, you have built no equity and have nothing to show for your money except, perhaps, years of low stress and peace of mind—and that may be what you want.

If, on the other hand, your first priority is to build equity, you should look for modest housing, perhaps the smallest, most simple house on a nice street in an area with potential for economic growth. If you can come up with the down payment, you begin to build equity immediately through your mortgage payments, the interest on which is tax deductible. However, in order to make it worth your while financially, you must stay even with or ahead of inflation. That is, the value of your house must increase at a rate higher than the rate of inflation. In uncertain economic times, that may be difficult. On the other hand, even in uncertain economic times, there may be bargains available. Some people have simply gotten in over their heads with debt and need to sell in a hurry. Others need to relocate quickly to take advantage of employment opportunities. If you are the buyer in such a situation, you may find a bargain that can be a worthwhile investment.

Investing in vacation property. An investment in vacation property, if properly handled, can be an investment in your future and provide either income at the time you decide to sell or a retirement residence if you're planning to vacate your primary residence.

On the other hand, if the economy is volatile or in a downturn, vacation property is hit fast and hard. When people have to make choices about where to spend available money, one of the first things to go is the second house. Since many second homes are in vacation areas or resort areas, a whole area can be hard hit and property values can quickly plummet 20 percent or more. It is a mistake to look on vacation property as a way to make fast money. In our current economy, you might hold your own and gradually increase the worth of your property, but making a short-term killing can be extremely difficult.

If you have bought your second home primarily to test an area for future retirement, you may decide to ride out any real estate slump. It may be more valuable to you to have several years' experience living in an area during all four seasons to assess its appropriateness for your upcoming retirement than to make a real estate killing.

Living in investment real estate. One way to have it both ways is to own a two- or three-family dwelling in which you can live essentially rent-free. Ideally, all of your carrying costs for property taxes, mortgage, insurance, maintenance, and utilities are covered by the rent payments you collect on the other units. Shopping for such a property is complex and needs to be handled with great caution. It's essential to research whether current tenants in the selected building will stay and, if not, how likely you are to find new ones. You should also assess the economic condition of the neighborhood in general by reviewing the number of building vacancies, area cleanliness, incidence of loitering, and the flow of people in and out of businesses.

Nevertheless, if you proceed carefully, owning a home with a rental property can be an especially attractive arrangement. Your housing costs are essentially eliminated, and you build equity in an investment that may well pay off in both the short and long term.

Housing for dependents. If you have a dependent parent or parents or young adult children, you might want to consider investing in a modest two-, three-, or four-unit dwelling so that you can afford to cover their housing costs while still generating an income on your investment through a growth in equity. You might arrange to make a small down payment and take out a mortgage and then have your dependent manage the building for you. This can save you quite a lot of money in terms of staff costs and also give you peace of mind in that you know that someone you trust is in charge. If things go well, you can pay your dependent a salary for his or her efforts and deduct it as a business expense.

Checklist for leasing your property. If you are planning to rent your house or apartment, the items listed below must be included in the lease you and your tenant sign.

- Name, address, and phone number of landlord
- Name, address, and phone number of tenant
- Business name, address, and phone number of tenant
- Bank name, address, and account number of tenant
- Term of the lease
- Monthly and yearly rent amount
- Security deposit required
- Broker fee to be paid, where applicable
- Exact definition of space to be rented
- Responsibility for utilities such as heat, electricity, telephone
- Responsibility for repairs required during term of lease
- Detailed information regarding insurance existing on property and effect on tenant
- Limited definition of liability of landlord
- Remedy in case of default by tenant
- Detailed definition of furnishings, if applicable
- Transferability or nontransferability of lease
- Restrictions on pets
- Rights regarding keys to dwelling

- Restrictions on cars
- Restrictions on number of cotenants
- Information regarding name, address, and phone number of attorney for landlord and attorney for tenant

28

YOUR REAL ESTATE
NEEDS AND
EXPERTS

If you are looking for a house, you will probably go through a real estate agent. This can save you enormous amounts of time, particularly if you know what you are looking for. A good real estate agent will not waste your time by showing you houses that are hopelessly out of your price range, too large or too small, or simply not the style you want. You must, however, say just what it is you want, and what you are flexible about. If no stairs is a necessity but a fourth bedroom is only something you think would be nice to have, a good real estate agent won't show you a three-story house just because it has the extra bedroom.

If you are buying a house, a lawyer is a necessity. Even if you are renting, it is a good idea to review the documents with your lawyer. Standard lease and mortgage documents are notoriously one-sided in favor of the lessor or mortgagor. Your lawyer may be able to balance that one-sidedness by reducing your liability, giving you more time to carry out your required activities, or spreading out some of the payments.

If you are going to buy, check out two or three banks before contracting for your mortgage, because terms can vary greatly from bank to bank. If you've had a long-standing personal relationship with a bank, however, you may wish to place your mortgage there. Such a bank will usually give you a better deal than one at which you are unknown. Banks like to be your sole banker, handling all of your banking needs. If you have a solid track record and are trusted, you are more likely to be given every possible benefit.

29

INSURANCE

Adequate insurance is your safety net. Health insurance is your hedge against high health costs. Disability insurance protects you against a disability, major or minor, that puts you out of work and without a regular income for a period of time. Life insurance insures that your heirs will be able to enjoy a lifestyle close to that which you had provided for them. Property insurance guards against damage to or loss of property. Personal liability insurance protects you if someone has a mishap or accident while on your property or while using your property. Many other kinds of insurance, such as car insurance, cover special needs.

This is an area where an insurance broker can be helpful. Some brokers handle several different companies, and others deal with only a single company. They all want to sell you insurance, so it is a good idea to talk to several before you settle on one. Explain what your situation is and listen to their suggestions.

Overspending on insurance. It is common for people to have too much life insurance, not enough health insurance, and no disability insurance. Review what you're spending on insurance and how it's apportioned with your insurance broker, and be sure that you're actually meeting your real needs.

Insurance brokers. Your insurance broker should assist you in the formulation of an insurance plan that covers your currrent and future needs and those of your dependents. Your needs will change as time goes by. Your broker should review with you annually your health insurance, life insurance, disability insurance, property insurance, automobile insurance, and any career- or business-related insurance. Your insurance broker should also review your retirement plans, including life insurance, annuities, and trusts.

Insurance brokers receive their fee from the insurance companies for which they sell policies. It is your business to inquire as to the size of that fee and how it is handled.

Comparison shopping. Before you buy any kind of insurance, you should meet with an insurance broker you know and trust or who is recommended by someone you know and trust. Review the kinds of policies available for your needs, and inquire about the health of the company sponsoring these policies. There are several directories, such as *Best's Annual Insurance Directory,* that rate insurance companies in terms of their financial health and ability to make good on claims; it's worth checking them as well. Insurance is an important investment, and you should treat it as such.

Never sign up for any kind of insurance policy that someone attempts to sell you in a cold phone call. In all such inquiries, always ask for something in writing, then review the document with your lawyer, accountant, or other adviser.

30

HEALTH INSURANCE

You must have health insurance coverage that takes care of you for everything from routine and minor illnesses and injuries to catastrophic long-term illnesses. There are hundreds of variations on health insurance policies, and it is essential to put yourself through the tedious task of reading about each type that is available to you.

First of all, assess what kind of insurance you have through your employer or the employer of your spouse. You should set out to cover on your own those areas in which your existing coverage is inadequate. If you or your spouse loses your employment and consequently your health income, you should know that the COBRA law requires that the insurance company convert your corporate policy and let you make payments for up to 18 months while you seek other coverage. Having no insurance constitutes simply too great a risk; it is better to have some coverage, possibly with a relatively high deductible, than none at all.

New alternatives in health insurance include health maintenance organizations and preferred-provider organizations. These organizations attempt to take the highs and lows out of health care by covering all your health needs for one annual fee. The catch is that you probably have to use their doctors and their hospitals and you may lose a long-time relationship with a personal physician. You may also experience delays and inconveniences and find your hospital stays cut short.

The advantage is cost: comprehensive private health insurance for a woman and her dependents can cost anywhere from $1,500 to $5,000 a year, depending on the area and the deductible. The cost of an HMO, on the other hand, is usually between $1,000 and $2,000 a year.

You may feel that your medical needs are adequately covered by insurance available through your employer. That may be the case for now. However, the long-range prognosis is that employee insurance will be inadequate. First of all, many corporations have been gradually cutting back on medical benefits across the board for the last decade, while gradually increasing the contribution required by the employee.

At the same time, corporate America is visibly unstable. Years of mergers, acquisitions, downsizing, and plant closings, added to a shift from a product to a service economy, has left 30 percent of the American population with no health insurance. Workers in service industries are generally not unionized, leaving them vulnerable when companies cut back on the benefits offered. In addition, corporations are increasingly reducing their full-time staffs in favor of large numbers of part-time people who receive no benefits at all.

If you find yourself in a situation where your company simply ceases to exist, such as in a bankruptcy proceeding, you will quickly discover that the cost of funding your own insurance is very high. There is a law, the COBRA law, that requires that you be protected for a fixed period of time while you pay for insurance policies previously provided by an employer, but this coverage ultimately runs out and is expensive to convert.

Studies have shown that people without health insurance receive inferior health care. In many cases they simply don't seek medical attention when they need it because they feel they can't pay for it.

There are alternatives to private insurers, such as health maintenance organizations and preferred-provider organizations. These are interesting and less expensive alternatives in which you pay an annual fee in return for guaranteed care of a certain level and frequency by doctors chosen by the organization. Currently, the range and the quality of the service of these organizations is wide.

You should not depend on the insurance of your spouse. That insurance could disappear if you separate or divorce, if there is turmoil at your spouse's employer, or if your spouse loses his employment.

If you need to obtain your own health insurance, you can look for information on insurance companies in *Best's Annual Insurance Directory,* which describes and rates all licensed insurance companies. Call several directly to have their representatives visit you to explain the policies they offer. You can also join insurance programs offered by professional organizations; these are worth looking into because the rates are lower than those for individual policies.

If you and your spouse are insured by different companies, you may find that you need both insurance policies because neither meets all your requirements.

Medicare and Medicaid. When you become eligible for Social Security you automatically become eligible for Medicare, which consists of medical insurance and hospital care insurance. These policies have deductibles, and neither covers all of your costs. You may wish to look into so-called MediGap insurance, which can pick up the difference between your real costs and those covered by Medicare. Be careful, however. The protection these policies offer varies considerably.

Medicaid, on the other hand, is medical coverage for all medical bills. It requires no copayments or deductibles and is available to those in financial need, such as those on federal assistance programs. You must meet stringent standards to be eligible for payments.

Clearly, you hope you will never need Medicaid and never be in a position where you qualify for it. But the future is impossible to predict.

Disability insurance. Disability insurance is perhaps the most important overlooked form of insurance. Your chances of becoming disabled before you reach 65 are much greater than your chances of dying before that age. Disability insurance comes in several formats, including disability payments made to you if you are totally or partially disabled or disabled enough so that you cannot perform your current professional job. Premiums vary according to the extent of coverage. You should have some sort of basic disability insurance, since something as common as an automobile accident can in six months' time wipe out your life savings.

31

LIFE INSURANCE

If you are single and have no dependents, you don't need life insurance. However, if you have any dependents at all, you should have at least some life insurance. The amount you need depends on other aspects of your financial planning, but a good rule of thumb is to have coverage equal to two to three times your annual income. If you have separate dependent children or dependent ill parents, you should increase your life insurance accordingly.

There are many types of life insurance policies. Term insurance provides basic coverage for the amount of the death benefit for a modest annual premium. Whole life insurance adds a savings feature; it builds up a cash balance in addition to providing life insurance. Whole life policies pay moderate interest, carry higher premiums, and can be borrowed against at low interest.

A third type of policy is the annuity, really a savings plan that pays benefits later during your life or after your death to a beneficiary. With an annuity, you can take a lump sum upon your retirement, receive monthly or annual payments during your lifetime, or have a payout again either in a lump sum or periodically, paid to a beneficiary after your death. Your broker should review your needs with you and structure your plan accordingly.

32

PROPERTY INSURANCE

Your possessions, including your home, should be fully insured against damage, theft, and fire. Such insurance carries a relatively low premium when it provides for only partial reimbursement for lost property. Most expensive, but better, is replacement value insurance, in which the insurance company pays the replacement cost of the goods lost. Your mortgage holder will insist that your home be insured for at least the value of the mortgage.

It is wise to make a video tape showing your dwelling and all your possessions, with an audio track in which you briefly describe the items and their value. This tape should be put in your safe deposit box to support any claim you may need to file. It is also wise to keep a permanent record of the serial numbers of any machines or appliances, as well as sales receipts for all important items.

You may wish to also take out fine arts coverage for important artwork or silver. Separate policies are also available for jewelry, furs, and boats. Automobile insurance is required if you own a car; you should discuss with your broker the proper amount for the type and age vehicle you drive.

Using appraisers. If you have invested in art, collectibles, jewelry, or silver, you will require the services of a licensed appraiser at least every two or three years. First, you should be current and accurate in your appraisal of these assets as they relate to your net worth. Second, you need to keep your insurance policies current, especially if they call for replacement value on these important items. You should make a videotape of all of your possessions, especially one-of-a-kind valuables, as backup for your insurance policies and store it in your safe deposit box, not in your home where it can be destroyed or stolen.

33

KEEPING GOOD RECORDS

Whether you are in corporate life, in professional practice, are self-employed, or are retired, you must assume responsibility for all of your business, legal, family, and medical dealings. It is essential to keep detailed, complete, accurate, and chronological records. Such records are the backbone of claims for benefits due you, dealing with insurance companies, prosecuting any kind of litigation, organizing your retirement, and, extremely important, predicting your future financial needs. Take the time to get organized and properly file all significant documentation, such as all tax returns filed as well as backup documentation for income and expenses; your will; all insurance policies; an inventory of all of your possessions (preferably video-taped as well); and personal papers, such as birth certificate, marriage certificate, divorce decree, custody papers, mortgages, leases, partnership agreements, brokerage records, invoices documenting major purchases and renovations, and automobile and boat registration.

All these documents can be kept in your safe deposit box with the following exceptions: The original of your will and insurance documents belong with your attorney, with photocopies in your safe deposit box. Your tax records belong with your accountant.

Checklist of personal papers. It is important to maintain an up-to-date list of personal papers. In the event of your disability or death or of a catastrophe such as hurricane or fire that destroys your home or business, you, your spouse, attorney, executor, or other person who needs access should know where to find important documents. When you update your list, make sure that

the current location of each item is updated as well.
Important papers include:
- Birth certificate
- Marriage certificate
- Separation agreement and/or divorce papers
- Custody decree
- Will
- All insurance policies
- Cemetery deed
- Social Security documents
- Military papers (discharge, etc.)
- List of all bank accounts
- List with account numbers of all credit cards
- Ownership documents for stocks, bonds, mutual funds, and other investments
- Documents regarding retirement plans
- All business contracts regarding ownership, partnerships, and agent agreements
- Receipts for major household and personal possessions
- Automobile, airplane, or boat registrations

34

THOSE YOU LIVE WITH

Whether you live alone or with a child or children, a companion, a spouse, or older dependents such as parents, you have certain legal responsibilities and liabilities. In this section, I discuss the obligations that go along with sharing your home with a companion or spouse.

The legal basis and ultimate outcome of living arrangements involving a companion or spouse are no longer predictable or simple. If you are married, you are subject to state laws governing property ownership and how property is to be divided in the event of a divorce; insurance policy disposition; child guardian and custody arrangements; alimony and temporary support payments (either husband to wife or wife to husband); and joint ownership of real estate, investments, employment benefits, and government benefits.

· *Every* married couple should have a premarital or post-marital agreement that covers the basics. This document serves as an insurance policy and eliminates controversy and possible litigation should the marriage be dissolved. It also establishes, in writing, the financial objectives and understandings of both parties. Matrimonial litigation is an unpredictable area of law, and similar cases do not necessarily have similar outcomes; state laws vary widely, as do individual judges' interpretations of existing laws. The process of matrimonial litigation is extremely slow, and it is not uncommon for a case to take many years to make its way through the courts, carrying high legal and accounting fees and devastating psychological and emotional impact. Because of these considerations, it is foolish not to pin down in writing at the outset a settlement of the questions that might arise later in any separation or divorce.

If you are not married but are living with a companion, you are not necessarily any better off. Companions do have financial rights, and there are real questions regarding property ownership. In addition, there is increasing custody litigation between unmarried live-in companions. You would be wise to work with your attorney to reach a written agreement with your live-in companion to cover areas likely to be in dispute should you split up. Be wary of signing leases or agreeing to joint ownership of credit cards, bank accounts, real estate, or automobiles. Untangling such agreements can be very difficult.

Even if you are not married, separated, or engaged, you can find yourself in legal and financial trouble if a person with whom you have been living chooses to sue you for support, possessions, business ownership, or even health benefits. This is a case where you need to know your rights. It is absolutely essential that you keep detailed records of your contributions if you are living with someone with whom you share financial obligations. Obviously, you should maintain separate bank accounts; less obviously, you should insist that special clauses be inserted in leases and mortgages to protect you if your relationship breaks up.

35

DIVORCE

In addition to emotional devastation, divorce carries the potential for financial devastation. With the divorce rate for first marriages hovering around 50 percent and the rate for second and third marriages even worse, it is prudent to be prepared for the possibility that your marriage may not succeed.

The days when the woman got the children, the house, and lifetime alimony payments are over. If you are thinking of marriage, you should familiarize yourself with the divorce law in your state. First of all, be sure to have a will that clearly expresses your wishes. Second, despite the notion that they are "unromantic," having prenuptial agreements is smart. If you and your husband view your life together as a partnership, then you should be able to spell out in a prenuptial agreement how you would divide any savings, investments, pension plans, real estate, and business ownership.

One of the most traumatic developments in any divorce is a dispute between the spouses over a business one of them has started. Entrepreneurs tend to view their businesses like children; they love and nurture them. It's bad enough to face the prospect of having to sell your business, but it can be truly horrendous to think that your ex-husband might get all or part of it.

Try to place a value on important nontangible items, such as your spouse's medical practice, contributions you have made to your spouse's medical school costs or the cost of other advanced degrees, and the worth of legal or accounting practices, business interests, and pension plans. It is generally easier if your lawyer and your spouse's work out details of your prenuptial agreement, since discussions between you and your spouse may become overly emotional.

If this marriage is your second or third, you may well have certain priorities that are not shared by your new husband. These may include your commitment to children from a previous marriage, your parents, maybe even friends and associates. Anyone entering a second or third marriage should surely have a prenuptial agreement that protects her unique interests should the marriage fail.

36

BANKS AND
BANKERS

Your bank is much more than a place to keep cash. It can provide a mortgage for a house, finance a renovation or a college education, set up a trust, and serve as executor or coexecutor of your estate. In addition, many banks have investment divisions that can help you establish a program of savings and investments.

You should become familiar with all of the services your bank offers and meet the heads of the appropriate departments. Take advantage of all services that are useful now and keep in mind that others may be useful in the future. A long-term good relationship with a bank will be a major asset throughout your life. If, for instance, at some point you decide to start your own business and you have had a decade or two of good dealings with your bank, that should be the first place you go for your start-up funds. A bank that views you as a long-time customer with a solid track record is much more likely to accommodate you than is a bank at which you are a total stranger.

Chances are that you deal with a branch of a major banking system that can meet all of your banking needs, including a checking account, a safe deposit box, a savings account, a NOW SWEEP account (which moves your money around to make sure that you are earning top interest), an investment account for handling CDs and treasuries, and a money market account. Your bank is also equipped to finance a mortgage for you to purchase a home or refinancing an existing mortgage. Finally, it may have a business lending division that can fund your business start-up or business partnership.

Your Banker. You should consult your banker about all financial transactions, including mortgages, leases, business start-ups, purchases and sales, loans, and major investments. Your banker can advise you on the cost of money, the best way to finance any purchase, and what your interest cost will be if you decide to borrow.

Your banker is also an excellent source of information as you try to stay ahead of inflation.

37

BORROWING

Debt is a burden and should be avoided when possible. Although buying a house and taking a 30-year mortgage may be a good idea, it is rarely smart to run up a lot of credit card debt. While credit cards are convenient, the interest charged on them is very high (averaging 18 percent) and will cost you considerably more than it would simply to borrow the money for a needed major item and pay bank interest on it. There was a time when interest on personal debt was tax-deductible, making the high interest payments a bit more palatable; however, that deduction has been phased out as a result of the 1986 Tax Reform Act.

It is a good idea to establish a credit line at a bank, borrow against it when you need it, and repay it promptly. This helps to establish both a solid credit rating and a solid relationship with the bank. (The line of credit should not be used, of course, unless necessary.)

To establish a line of credit, you need to meet with your banker to decide on an appropriate credit limit, taking into consideration your income, expenses, age, occupation, and liquid assets. A line of credit is best used for important and necessary purchases for which funds are not readily available. For instance, you might want to use it to purchase a car (although there are other loan options for automobiles), to pay tuition, or to meet a medical emergency.

Checklist for credit application. The following is a listing of those items you can expect to find on all applications for loans and credit:
- Name
- Date of birth
- Current address

- Telephone number
- Previous address
- Social Security number
- Name, address, and phone number of nearest relative not living with you
- Name, address, and phone number of employer
- Number of years with employer
- Position and title
- Same information for previous employer
- Current income including salary and commissions
- Alimony and child support received
- Business partnership distributions or dividends, agent's fees
- Listing of current bank accounts, including checking, savings, other
- Listing of all credit cards with current balance and account number
- All mortgages, including primary residence, second home, investment real estate
- Name of bank, account number, amount of mortgage, year mortgage issued, average monthly payment due
- Automobile—type, year, registration number, and average monthly car loan or leasing payment

If you are seeking a large loan (such as to finance a business start-up), a complete net worth statement will be required. A sample net worth statement is included in Key 6.

Credit. There are a number of federal laws that protect you when you borrow money or use credit, and you should be familiar with them.

The *Equal Credit Opportunity Act* guarantees that you cannot be denied a loan on the basis of sex, race, or marital status.

The *Truth in Lending Act* requires that any lender make the following information clear to the borrower:
- The finance charge and any "hidden" items like annual fees
- Late payment penalties
- The total amount really being borrowed, including interest, and the total number of payments required

- A description of the method by which the interest rate is set

The *Fair Credit Reporting Act* gives you the right to know the name and address of any credit agency reporting credit data on you and to review the information. If you find errors, you have the right to notify the agency and seek correction. If an agency has improperly made available incorrect credit information about you, it is then required to send the new, corrected information to anyone who received the erroneous information. Furthermore, accurate negative credit information about you cannot be supplied for more than seven years, except in the case of bankruptcies, which can be reported for fourteen years.

Several other laws also impact on credit and collection practices. These include various amendments to the Equal Credit Opportunity Act protecting the elderly and minorities, in special circumstances; the *Federal Garnishment Law,* which limits the amount your employer can withhold from your paycheck because of liens against your salary; and the *Collection Practices Act,* which protects you from harassment by debtors should you be unable to make timely payments on your debts. For instance, bill collectors are prohibited from calling you on the telephone before 8 AM or after 9 PM.

The Federal Trade Commission in Washington, D.C. 20580 publishes a number of pamphlets regarding borrowing, including one entitled "Women and Credit Histories."

38

CREDIT COUNSELORS

If you find that you are in financial difficulty, it is best not to try to tough it out or go it alone. Even if you have used a financial planner, investment adviser, and real estate adviser, you still may find that you cannot handle your debt because of unemployment, illness, or other unpredictable circumstances. All of your creditors are entitled to be paid on time, and in all cases where credit has been extended to you, you will have signed a document guaranteeing payment. Most of the creditors (with the exception of the bank holding your mortgage and possibly your car loan) permit you to run thirty days late on any given payment, especially if your record has been good. Once you are forty-five days late on a payment, you generally hear through the mail or through a telephone call from your creditor. After sixty days, the inquiries from your creditors become more intense, and you may at this point be threatened with some sort of legal action. After ninety days that legal action is likely to begin. At this point your delinquencies will have been reported to your credit bureau and will appear on your credit rating. Ninety-day delinquencies are considered very serious.

Before you get to this point (preferably a month or two earlier), you should seek the advice of a credit counselor. There are credit counselors who work on a fee basis; for those in dire straits, there are city and state agencies that provide credit counseling free.

A credit counselor will take several steps. First, he or she will notify all of your creditors that you have a credit counselor, that you are eager to meet your obligations, and that your counselor will prepare in each case a proposed repayment schedule that will allow you to begin to repay your debts.

If your difficulty is truly temporary, such intervention by a counselor will generally clear up your problem. The counselor will work with you to prepare a budget that meets your basic monthly needs, eliminates all optional and luxury items, and allows for installment payments on overdue debt.

It is preferable, however, for you to contact each of your creditors personally at the first sign of serious trouble. If you alert creditors that you will be two weeks or a month or two late with a payment, they will generally suspend your credit privileges but give you the extra time to pay. If you, on the other hand, ignore all of their inquiries and disregard their warnings, in many cases they can hold you in default and call you on payment of the total amount you owe.

Even if you have managed to work out some arrangement with your creditors, you might still want to consult a credit counselor to help you prepare a budget and avoid future problems.

39

MANAGING YOUR HOUSEHOLD

Whether you are married or single, whether you have four children or no children, and whether you have a dependent live-in parent, your household needs managing. This is a job many women handle themselves in addition to their jobs or careers. However, those who can afford it often hire help. Obviously, the more complex your responsibilities, the more help you need.

If you can afford it, your needs will probably be best met by a professional household manager, a top-of-the-line person who is generally familiar with housekeeping, cooking, child care, and dependent adult care and who either handles all of these responsibilities herself or hires and supervises the additional staff you need, depending on the size of your household and your specific needs. For instance, you may require help with general housekeeping, grocery shopping, cooking, care of one or more school-age children, business entertaining four times a month, holiday coordination and shopping, and general supervision of repair and maintenance people. The household manager might oversee all of these activities with the assistance of a maid who comes once or twice a week, a cook who comes for all business entertaining, an afternoon babysitter who picks your children up at school and takes them to lessons, appointments, and playdates, and a senior citizen assistant who provides recreational activities for an aging parent once or twice a week.

Professional household managers can be found through major domestic employment agencies operating in all major cities and many suburban areas. Unfortunately, the cost of a household manager is unlikely to be tax deductible.

If you are fortunate enough to have a competent household manager, you will have a constant presence in your household and the peace of mind that comes from knowing that all of your important bases are covered by someone who is trustworthy and competent.

For the professional woman who travels, some sort of household management is not a luxury but a necessity.

Dealing with repair and maintenance staff. From time to time you will require the services of various repair and maintenance workers, from plumbers and electricians to gardeners and landscapers. Regardless of the circumstance, there are certain general rules to follow.

First, deal only with licensed practitioners. If you use someone who is not licensed, you have no recourse if something goes wrong. On the other hand, if you have a problem with a licensed supplier, you can always take your complaint to his trade organization. For example, if a licensed plumber proves incompetent, you have recourse to the licensing agency.

Second, always seek competing bids. Many contractors arrive at their estimates for a job based on "what the traffic will bear." This rarely works to your advantage. You should always get two or three *written* bids for all work you require.

Third, don't pay in full up front. It is reasonable for all contractors to require some payment at the inception of the work, but thereafter you should pay as the work progresses.

You should hold contractors to their estimates for supplies as well as for the time required to complete the job. If supplies are running over budget or the project is running late, withhold payment until the matter is resolved.

Finally, before hiring any outside workers, always ask for and check out references and contact local licensing agencies to see if there are any unresolved complaints pending against the worker.

40

MEETING YOUR PSYCHOLOGICAL NEEDS

As a working woman, you compete and work with men every day. In the workplace, you are all expected to play by the same rules, meet the same requirements, spend the same amount of time, and bring the same single-mindedness and confidence to your business activities.

If you never marry and have no children, this is probably a fair deal. If, on the other hand, you are married, or were married, or have children, the deck is really stacked against you. You have large, sometimes overwhelming responsibilities other than those of your professional life. Perhaps even more important, you probably do not have the full-time support and assistance of a "wife." Although you may be adept at putting together a network of household help—managers, nannies, cooks, housekeepers, drivers, and personal secretaries—you still have to coordinate and manage all of these employees. This is very different from having a spouse at home to manage these tasks for you with total dependability.

Don't try to go it alone. Take advantage of the innumerable professional and lay groups that have developed for professional women. Talking with other women at your professional level who are facing similar demands and responsibilities can be extremely helpful.

You may find that other women in your group have confronted and successfully dealt with the same difficulties you must now resolve, and you can benefit from their experience.

If participation in various professional organizations and their support groups does not provide relief from the stress you are enduring, by all means seek the assistance of a trained psychologist or psychiatrist. Serious stress can lead to a wide variety of problems, including serious medical ailments. Stress can also lead to professional burnout—a feeling of general malaise, a difficulty in going about your daily business, and a sense that your professional life is not worthwhile, that you will not succeed, and that your achievements don't matter. Burnout emotionally immobilizes you.

Inevitably, you will come face to face with the popular concept of "having it all." There is considerable pressure on professional women to combine their professional achievements with (frequently multiple) marriages, childbirth and child rearing, and caring for dependent parents. A professional woman is supposed to be able to handle all of this and remain startlingly fit, attractive, and sane.

It is possible to achieve a lot of this and remain serene. The trick appears to be to do it sequentially. It is extraordinarily difficult, if not impossible, to focus completely on your professional life while going through pregnancy, childbirth, and the early childhood years, or separation, divorce, or remarriage.

The women who make it through these minefields tend to concentrate on one thing at a time, making sure that the other fronts are stabilized. Progress on all fronts simultaneously is unlikely; don't expect it of yourself. This may mean that sometimes your career will have to take a back seat to other concerns that are for a time more pressing.

41

TIME SAVERS

Grooming requirements. If your profession requires your frequent presence at speaking engagements or client presentations, or if you appear on television, you will need the services of a competent beauty salon that can meet your hairdressing and other needs when *you* need them met. Perhaps your schedule makes it necessary for you to have all such appointments before 9 AM or after 6 PM or even on the weekends. Many beauty salons do not have facilities open at the times when you need them, and you may have to make an arrangement with a beauty professional on your own. This is not a frivolous expenditure; you are expected to be well groomed for all professional engagements.

The fitness adviser. As you go about meeting your professional obligations, you are surely working hard, putting in long hours, and juggling many roles. You are probably not getting enough exercise, and you are probably not eating properly because of time constraints. These practices are bad for you personally and professionally.

Engaging a fitness adviser, whether a personal trainer or a staff person at a fitness facility, is a good investment of your time and money. If you don't feel well or find your energy level sinking and your appearance deteriorating, the effect on your professional standing could be dramatic. Your judgment may be affected, your ability to communicate may suffer, and the example you set for others will be less than inspiring.

The "baby boom" generation grew up barraged by useful information regarding fitness, but older women did not benefit from the same kind of emphasis. It is difficult to take responsibility for one's fitness program, and easy to put it off.

A fitness program need not be terribly expensive. If money is no object, you may decide to hire a personal trainer who will customize a program that fits your personal needs and timetable. If that is not possible, any number of good fitness facilities will customize a fitness program for you for a modest fee. What they can't do is discipline you to attend their sessions and classes. This is an area that deserves serious thought and that you should make a personal priority.

The professional shopper. Many department stores make personal shoppers available to customers whose annual purchases at the store, exceed a certain amount, perhaps $1,000 or $2,000. These personal shoppers can save you an enormous amount of time by becoming familiar with your shopping patterns, and especially your clothing needs. They know if you need to dress for different climates because of business travel, if you are frequently a public speaker, or if you require clothing that is appropriate for particular purposes, such as television appearances. If they're good, personal shoppers make it their business to understand which designers and manufacturers produce clothing that is particularly flattering to you, and they make preliminary selections on a seasonal basis.

More mundane items that need replacing, such as hosiery, shoes, and pocketbooks, can be handled completely by the personal shopper. Remember, stores do not charge for this important service, which can help you look your best and make your purchases at the most advantageous time and price.

Travel agents. It has never been easy to deal with airlines, hotels, and car rental operations, and it seems particularly difficult now, as companies are in constant flux because of mergers, bankruptcies, and downsizing. At a time when constantly changing prices, overbookings, and cuts in service personnel are a given, it seems prudent to seek the services of a travel agency that is fully computerized and has ready access to up-to-date timetables, pricing schedules, and information on the availability of accommodations and rental cars.

Travel agents work on a commission; naturally their commission goes up if the price of tickets or accommodations is high *or* if they handle a large volume of reservations. If you use a travel agent in conjunction with a corporate group or a charitable group that does a lot of business with the travel agent, you will probably get better service and better bottom-line deals. However, even if you come out financially right where you would have been had you made your own reservations, you will have saved a lot of time by using a travel agent. It is important to monitor travel agents, at least at first, to be sure that they have offered you all of the possibilities in airline reservations, hotel reservations, and car leasing reservations so that you can make the final choice as to which is easiest and most economical for you. Then you can establish a long-term relationship with a travel agent who becomes familiar with your requirements, preferences, and schedule and who can anticipate many of your needs.

42

YOUR RETIREMENT

For purposes of this book, I assume that you have been gainfully employed, that you will at some point retire from that employment or business, and that you are funding your own retirement. The first thing to keep in mind is that for many women who entered the work force late, their retirement years will exceed the number of years they were gainfully employed. Life expectancy has been increasing every year, and the old-fashioned notion that people retired at 65 and then "had a few good years" is now viewed as nonsense. Women work productively into their seventies and even eighties, especially those who own their own businesses or who are part of an unregulated profession, such as the law.

It is best to view retirement as a gradual reduction in the number of hours worked, perhaps from ten hours a day to eight hours to six hours to whatever is manageable.

Retirement needs to be planned for on more than one front. You naturally are concerned with the amount of money that will be available to you in partial or full retirement, but you should also know about those employment fields that will be open to you in your fifties and on. If you are currently a fashion model, for instance, faced with the prospect of being "over the hill" at 27, it would be best to plan early for a second career.

Many fields have a predictable age at which opportunities begin to dwindle, but there are, happily, other fields, such as teaching, writing, counseling, and consulting, in which opportunities grow with experience and age is viewed as a plus. It obviously also makes sense to look at areas in the economy that are growing now and that will still be growing when you near retirement age. Obvious examples are companies concerned with the environment, all services for an aging population, and firms involved in international trade. A careful retirement plan lays out employment or business start-up opportunities and details what is required to take advantage of these opportunities.

Retirement also means looking carefully at your housing needs. If you had a large family at home but no longer do, you will probably want to consider a smaller dwelling that is easier to care for.

Although the lure of a warm climate and beautiful golf courses is real, research shows that retired people who move far away from their families and friends frequently regret it and move back. In retirement, family and friends and comfortable surroundings provide a major support system.

You may have acquired a weekend or vacation home in an area where retirement might be appealing. If you've planned carefully, you will have assessed area in terms of employment or new business start-up opportunities for retired people, income levels, medical facilities, school taxes, zoning restrictions, and rate of real estate appreciation.

Of course, you must first decide whether you wish to retire and whether it's even a good idea to retire. Many surveys indicate that people who are working, even part-time, are happier and healthier and live longer. Retirement to a beach or golf course and the prospect of doing nothing may look terrific now, but when you reach 65 you may have other thoughts.

In addition, you might not be able to afford to retire. It is generally assumed that you will require approximately two-thirds of your current income if you retire at age 65. Considering increases in longevity and the prospect that you may live into your eighties or even nineties, you can see you will need to save and invest a substantial amount of money every year for most of your productive working life to finance even a twenty-year retirement.

American Association of Retired Persons. The American Association of Retired Persons (AARP) is an enormous organization open to Americans age 50 and over.

For a very modest membership fee, the AARP provides members with a vast array of information regarding retirement, including employment opportunities and rights, insurance needs, housing, leisure, investments, and health care.

Reviewing AARP retirement planning material should be of great interest to people at age 30. They can spend twenty years benefiting from all of the good advice the material contains. In this way, by the time they retire, whether at 50 or later, they will already have done the basic groundwork for a successful retirement.

43

RETIREMENT EXPENSES

To help anticipate how your costs will change after you retire, list the major expenses you face now and compare them to those you expect to face in retirement. You will probably include housing (rent or mortgage on primary residence), possibly a vacation home, car payments and insurance, education costs for children, any contribution you're now making to your parents, insurance and health costs, continuing education costs, travel and entertainment costs, investments for long-term goals, and savings.

You should review ways in which your situation will change when you retire. If your children will be grown and you feel you will no longer need your weekend or vacation residence, you can eliminate the costs of supporting your children, paying tuition, and keeping up your weekend vacation home from your projection. You might decide to sell your current large house and buy something smaller and less costly, further reducing expenses.

As you age, however, you can expect your health and insurance costs to rise, and you probably need to budget more for leisure activities than you now spend. If you are investing to cover the costs of several decades of retirement, you may need to start setting aside more for that investment portfolio than you currently do.

Tax implications of retirement. Every major decision you make while planning for retirement has tax implications. For instance, different states handle taxation of income and pension fund payouts differently. Be sure you know the laws in your state, and any you are considering moving to. In addition, any transfer of property to your children at this point has tax implications; be sure to do it in the most advantageous way, after consulting both your lawyer and your accountant.

Quality of life. Although this is not a book about fitness, it is appropriate to mention that one of the best investments you can make for your retirement is in your health and fitness. Have annual checkups, follow the advice of your doctor regarding proper eating, exercise properly, and get enough rest. Retirement is more pleasant and far less expensive, and employment in retirement is more of a pleasure and challenge, for those who are fit.

44

RETIREMENT MYTHS

Although many old theories regarding retirement are simply no longer useful, it's hard to part with them and the relative security they provided. For instance, at one time you could assume that your home would continuously increase in value and that you could borrow against its value or sell it at retirement to provide funds to invest and finance a comfortable retirement. The reality of the current housing market is that for the foreseeable future, housing is likely either to maintain its current value or to drop in value. (In some markets, real estate values have dropped 20 to 30 percent during the last several years.) Homeowners may face the nasty situation of finding that their equity is less than the debt they owe on their home; the selling price may be lower than the outstanding mortgage and home equity loan against it.

Another myth that dies hard is that Social Security will cover all of your basic expenses. This is certainly not the case, and it was never in fact intended to be the case. Social Security was always meant simply to put a floor under the income level of older Americans so that they would not slip into poverty. Social Security benefits are modest, and most people are unable to live on those benefits alone.

Yet another myth claims that your pension will cover all your needs. If you are lucky enough to have a pension, you will probably find that it covers less than you thought. If you take a lump sum payment upon retirement, the money is likely to vanish rather quickly if it is not invested in instruments that outperform inflation. If you take a long-term payout, you may find that your standard of living is seriously curtailed.

In the worst of all possible scenarios, your pension simply vanishes because your previous employer goes bankrupt, is involved in some sort of banking fraud, or for other reasons. Although there are laws to protect your pension in such cases, the situation is not foolproof, and you may end up with nothing.

Yet another myth is the one that says that your former employer will pay all of your medical bills forever. This theory is perhaps the shakiest. Employers are confronting skyrocketing health costs, and in many cases they feel they cannot carry the health bills of increasing numbers of retired people as well as those currently employed. There is much negotiation going on behind the scenes to find ways to reduce or eliminate benefits to retirees. This is especially critical to the elderly, since the health needs of people past retirement age are usually much greater than those of younger people.

It's also kidding yourself to rely on your health insurance, pension, and Social Security. Maybe they will in fact be enough to protect you. But then again maybe they won't. There are several factors at work that diminish the certainty of this kind of arrangement. First of all, divorce is increasingly common among older people; you should find out what benefits you would be eligible for from your husband's pension, corporate health policy, and Social Security coverage in the event of a divorce. You should also find out what your entitlements would be should your husband predecease you or should his company merge or cease to do business. It is not pleasant to look into these unpleasant possible eventualities, but you owe it to yourself to plan for even unpleasant possibilities.

A final myth claims that your children will take care of you in your retirement. Again, maybe they will. On the other hand, it is likely that your children will be part of the ever-growing "sandwich" generation that is saddled with the burden of young children, born later in the marriages, and aging parents, who live longer and are ill or disabled for significant portions of their later years. Although your children certainly may wish to undertake total responsibility for you in retirement, it may simply be impossible for them.

You should also consider the possibility that you may in fact be taking care of *your* parent or parents when you retire in your sixties. They may be well advanced in years or disabled, and may require expensive care for a number of years. It can be difficult to meet their needs as well as your own; careful planning for this eventuality is well advised if it is a possibility you may have to face.

Today's retirement reality. It is your responsibility to know the reality of your own retirement years and to plan for the likelihood that one or more of the benefits you are currently planning on will be eliminated or curtailed. You should also be prepared for other probabilities—that you will have to assume some responsibility for the care and expenses of an aging parent, perhaps after you yourself are of retirement age, and that you will need to supplement your own retirement benefits with outside income from an investment portfolio, insurance policies or annuities, your own business, or part-time work.

A large percentage of those living in poverty in the United States are elderly women. To protect yourself, you should begin to plan for your own retirement starting when you are in your thirties; by the time you're in your forties, you should have a relatively clear-cut idea of your options; and by the time you reach your fifties, you should be testing the water, perhaps with a small business on the side, changes in your insurance and real estate holdings, or a review of your investment portfolio.

45

WHAT TO DO NOW TO PLAN FOR RETIREMENT

To begin planning for your retirement, call your local Social Security office and ask them to send you their PEBES form. After you complete it and mail it in, the Social Security office will send you an estimate of your future Social Security benefits based on your contribution to date.

Next, if you are employed, talk to someone in your personnel or human resource department about your benefits. If your company has a pension plan, you should enroll if you have not already done so. You may be required to make a small contribution, which will be matched by your employer, out of your paychecks. When you retire, you will likely have a choice of receiving a lump sum payment or continuous payments during your retirement. Have your accountant work out the dollar value of both approaches before deciding.

Find out whether your company offers a 401-k or similar program through which you invest a certain amount of your gross pay each week or month, which may be matched by your employer. The money is professionally invested for you, and your contribution and income from investment are both tax-free until they are withdrawn after your retirement. These 401-k programs are very attractive and easy for your employer to administer. If there is no pension plan at your company, you might encourage it to begin a 401-k plan.

If you are self-employed, you should meet with your accountant to review the pros and cons of setting up a Keogh plan, which allows you to build a pension-like retirement fund. You should try to contribute the maximum to your Keogh to reduce your taxable income and to save as much as possible tax-free.

If you are not already saving, start now, even if you begin with only 5 percent of your net or, better yet, gross pay.

Review what medical and health benefits will be available to you upon retirement from your company. If there are options available to you, take the most comprehensive coverage possible. You should do the same with your company life insurance. Remember, you can get life insurance faster and cheaper when you are young.

Then meet with your insurance agent to review what policies you need to take out to supplement those available from your employer or your spouse's employer. Look to your long-range needs for life insurance, disability insurance, and health insurance. Your goal again is to buy insurance when it's easy to get and least expensive and to be assured of full coverage later in life.

If you have an investment portfolio, meet with your broker to review your long-range plan. You're probably willing to assume a greater amount of risk while you're relatively young than you will be as you enter your middle and later years. Make sure that your broker understands that you will expect income from your investments in your retirement years and that you will not be interested in taking a flyer on hot new offerings at that time.

Carefully review employer documents regarding plans for retirement, early retirement, pension, health care options, continuing education, and dependent care. Many people fail to take advantage of programs offered by their employers simply because they are unaware of them. It is your responsibility to check with your personnel department periodically to keep up to date on available benefits. If, for instance, your employer offers dependent care for your small children or your aging parents and you have need of this service, you should avail yourself of this benefit. If there is a generous early retirement package available, review it with your lawyer and accountant; sometimes packages look terrific at first glance but actually leave you with insufficient income a few years down the road.

One of the best possible situations for you, upon your retirement or even early retirement, is for you to continue in a part-time or consulting capacity for your employer after you officially retire. In some situations, you may be allowed to receive full health, insurance, and pension benefits as well as, obviously, continuing income.

If you have not worked previously and have been dependent upon your spouse's coverage, you should find out everything about all benefits available to him.

Some very large companies and some trade organizations offer interesting little-known benefits, such as special medical and wholesale drug-buying arrangements, low-interest loans, and discounts on senior citizen recreational and leisure activities. All of these are worth looking into.

46

ESTATE PLANNING

Estate planning is not a subject to deal with on your seventieth birthday. It needs your attention as soon as you begin to acquire assets and as soon as you have any dependents. Estate planning—the process by which you protect yourself and your assets throughout your employed life and during your retirement and protect your heirs at the time of your death—includes not only allocating your possessions and insurance among your heirs but also protecting them against unnecessary taxes.

Your personal estate plan should be reviewed with your attorney and probably your accountant at least once a year. These reviews will grow more complex as you marry, have children, assume some responsibility for aging parents, and face the realistic costs of your retirement and health care. It is complicated by the fact that 50 percent of first marriages and an even higher percent of second and third marriages end in divorce. The complexities of providing for your own children and one or more sets of stepchildren are enormous. If your family includes children by a previous marriage (yours or your husband's), it is unlikely that your wishes will be identical to his. Recognize this and deal with it with all proper precautions.

Your estate includes your personal and household possessions. But it also includes all benefits to which you are entitled through your current employer, previous employers, and the government, and perhaps part or all of a small business. Finally, it includes any insurance policies or trusts and all investments, such as stocks and bonds.

Current inventory of assets. It is important for you to keep a list of your assets and liabilities and to update it at least annually. Copies should be left with your attorney, with the executor of your will, and in your safe deposit box.

The following is a list of some of the items which you should include in your asset inventory:

- Residential real estate, including primary residence and second home
- Automobiles
- Boats, airplanes, recreational vehicles
- Fine art
- Jewelry, furs
- Home furnishings
- Silver, antiques
- Collectibles (anything from baseball cards and stamps to rare porcelains or dolls)
- All bank accounts (savings, checking, money market, NOW accounts)
- Insurance policies (including annuities)
- Employee benefits (profit sharing, 401-k plans)
- Stocks
- Bonds
- Mutual funds
- Money market funds
- Equity position in any business including your own

Inventory of personal and business debt obligations. This category includes the following items:

- Mortgages
- Personal loans
- Credit card balances
- Bank loans
- Taxes due

47

DIVIDING YOUR ESTATE

Even if you have determined that you wish to take care of four or five people in your estate planning, you should give serious consideration to *how* you include them. To simply take your net worth and divide it by five is probably not practical; alternate arrangements may well be advisable. Here's an example of how you might divide your estate, providing for everyone but protecting your assets as well. Assume your children from your first marriage are grown and that you want them to receive equal cash payments from your estate upon your death. Your second husband is slightly disabled and you want him to receive ongoing annual payments to cover his care, but because you don't feel he's the proper manager for the money, you have appointed a trustee. You also have a young child from your second marriage, and you want a substantial piece of your estate to be placed in trust for this child with a specified amount of money earmarked for education. You have appointed a trustee to oversee this, as well.

You own your own business but do not feel that either your second husband or your children from your first or second marriage are sufficiently interested in or knowledgeable about your business. You have therefore appointed a trustee to sell your business upon your death and divide the proceeds according to a predetermined formula. This trustee is particularly knowledgeable about the tax aspects of your business.

Finally, you have several long-term employees whom you wish to provide small life insurance policies, outside of your estate.

Trusts. There are innumerable kinds of trusts available to help you deal with your estate in a very sophisticated manner. Perhaps your goal is to provide income to a spouse, children, parents, employees, or friends. You can do this through an outright bequest or through a trust in which the income and interest earned by an asset are distributed to the beneficiary but the core asset is not; the asset may be passed to another beneficiary, perhaps a charity, at a later time. Trusts can be set up to cover the complexities created by multiple marriages stepchildren, loyal employees, and nonfamily dependents. There are trusts to finance educations, pay off mortgages, and buy businesses. Creating trusts is a complex area, but one worth becoming familiar with. Once you know what you want to do, you should consult the trust department at your bank, your attorney, or possibly your accountant or financial planner regarding the options open to you. Once you have made your decision, a legal document must be drawn, signed, and witnessed properly.

Needless to say, any trusts you establish should be reviewed every year to make sure that they still match your needs and those of your heirs.

Living wills. A living will is a document in which you issue instructions regarding medical treatment for you should you become terminally ill or totally disabled. You can specify what sort of medical treatment you want, what you don't want, and who should make decisions for you if you are unable to make them. There is a great deal of litigation regarding the validity of certain elements of living wills, and you should check with your attorney if you are considering executing one.

Giving something back. As a successful woman, you may feel considerable gratitude toward your alma mater, toward your community, or toward professional groups that have helped you along the way. It is certainly satisfying and pleasurable to be able to repay people and institutions in some way. You might make an annual pledge to your college or endow a particular program or course; donate your business skills or business products

110

or services to worthy institutions in your community; or simply give your time to your trade organizations. All of these charitable activities are worthwhile in themselves; however, you should not forget to take advantage of the appropriate tax deductions in each case. Your accountant can advise you on how to time these donations to derive the maximum tax benefit and what format to use to ensure their deductibility.

48

COST OF PROFESSIONAL SERVICES

In the following section, I list the costs you can expect to face in seeking each of the types of professional services outlined in this book. The fees listed here are those you are likely to be charged in a major metropolitan area. These prices represent the top range. In smaller cities, in the suburbs, and in rural areas, you can expect lower prices, generally tied to the local economy.

Lawyers. Lawyers charge by the hour; charges are highest for full partners in metropolitan-area law firms and lower for associates. The fees also vary by type of legal work required. One lawyer at a firm might charge you $175 an hour for routine matters (preparing a will, reviewing a lease or retirement plan), while another lawyer at the same firm who specializes in business start-ups might charge $200 per hour.

Matrimonial attorneys start at about $200 an hour, and the celebrities among them charge up to $400 an hour. Associates' time is generally billed at $75 to $100 per hour (associates generally concentrate on drafting legal papers and doing research).

The most expensive legal service is litigation. Litigators start at about $200 per hour and average perhaps $350 an hour. Litigators inevitably require the assistance of several associates who do the background work; the litigator does the court appearance.

Financial planners. Some financial planners do planning only as a sideline to another business, such as operating a stock brokerage firm. In such cases, they do not charge a fee for their advice, but they do earn a commission on the products they sell you. Certified financial planners, on the other hand, do not sell a product. They simply provide financial planning, for either a flat fee or an hourly fee. Depending on the complexity of your financial needs, a financial planner might charge you a flat $100 or $200 fee to assess your current finances or a fee of $75 to $100 per hour on an ongoing basis. Other financial planners work on an annual retainer of several thousand dollars and provide either a guaranteed minimum number of hours or an open-ended number of hours.

Bankers. Your banker is employed by your bank and does not generally charge any kind of fee for his or her services. The banker's job is to understand your banking needs and to sell you the various products and services of his or her bank that meet your needs. These banking services do have some sort of fee attached, which contributes indirectly to the banker's compensation.

Tax preparers. Tax preparers may be accountants or they may be salaried people employed and trained by tax-preparing firms. Although you do not pay the tax preparer directly, you do pay the tax-preparation company a flat fee, which may be as low as $50 for a very simple return or several hundred dollars or more for a return including several separate schedules.

Accountants. Independent accountants (those in private practice, rather than employed by a firm) either charge by the hour or set a flat fee for specified services. The flat-fee system is more common; an accountant might charge $100 to prepare a simple tax return, $500, $1,000, or more if he provides some form of tax planning and fills out a relatively complicated return.

Accountants associated with accounting firms work on a billing schedule similar to that of law firms. Simple accounting matters might be billed out at $100 per hour, while complicated accounting matters, especially those that involve audits or litigation, might be billed out at $200 or $300 an hour. Senior partners bill in the upper range, and junior partners and associates bill at $100 per hour or less.

Real estate brokers. A real estate broker will sell your house or apartment for a 6 percent commission. The brokerage may do this by itself or in cooperation with another brokerage, in which case they split the 6 percent fee. You do not pay the broker directly; instead, you pay the brokerage firm, which retains the lion's share of the fee and pays the rest to the individual broker.

While brokerage fees are not supposed to be negotiable, they most certainly are. In times of a real estate slump, and even at other times, a broker might be willing to take four or five percent if it means completing a sale.

If, on the other hand, you use the services of a rental agency, you will probably have to pay the broker's fee, which could be as high as one month's rent. This, too, is negotiable, and sometimes the lessor and lessee each pay half the fee. Other times, such as when the property is also for sale, the broker will work on some other kind of commission that takes into account both the rental and the sale commissions.

Mortgage brokers. If you have decided not to seek a mortgage through a bank but have turned to a mortgage broker instead, you will find that their services are very expensive. Although these fees are extremely negotiable and can depend on who referred you to the broker (such as an accounting firm or a law firm) and the amount of business that the broker does with you and your company, a fee of one half point (a point equals one percent of the amount borrowed) is common. Thus, on a $300,000 mortgage, one point equals $3,000; the mortgage broker's fee is probably $1500.

Insurance brokers. Insurance agents and brokers work on a commission. Fees vary according to the company, the amount of business you do, and the type of policy involved. Generally you pay the commission as part of your first year's premium on any policy; it's up to you to ask how much of your payment is in fact the commission.

Stockbrokers. Stockbrokers may be either full-fee brokers or discount brokers. Full-fee brokers handle all

114

stock transactions, manage your portfolio, and make buy and sell recommendations. Their fees are often negotiable.

Discount brokers only buy and sell at your directive; they do not provide advisory services. Their rates are lower.

Estate planners. Estate planning may be offered as a free or inexpensive service at your bank if the bank is going to act as the executor or coexecutor in your estate (for which it will earn a fee).

Law firms and accounting firms also offer estate planning, at their hourly rate.

Computer consultants. Computer consultants are a relatively new breed. Their rates are very definitely negotiable; fees start at about $50 an hour, although many consultants work on a flat-fee-for-installation basis.

As a rule of thumb, the more complex and advanced your computer, the more you will pay for the consultant's services.

Headhunters or the employment agencies. Headhunters work for corporate clients. They are really consultants who are brought in by corporate clients for from several months to a year to help companies fill important openings, generally at very senior levels. The headhunter is generally paid between 25 and 33 percent of the first year's compensation for the candidate being sought. The headhunter is paid whether or not the slot is filled by one of her candidates.

Headhunters generally agree that they will not raid the company for which they are doing a search in an effort to find candidates for other clients.

Employment agencies work very differently. They work for a company, in that they fill a vacancy the company lists with them, but they also work for the individual for whom they secure interviews at various companies. Customarily, the agency fee (typically one month's salary) is paid by the jobseeker for lower-level positions and split or picked up entirely by the company for higher-level positions.

Career counselors. Most career counseling is provided free, either through your university, your trade organization, your union, or your employer.

There are private career counselors, many of them with a degree in counseling. Their fees tend to be modest, in the range of $50 per hour. The best way to find a career counselor is certainly through word of mouth. If that route does not produce what you need, ask the advice of your personnel department head, the president of your trade organization or union, or the placement office of your alma mater.

Credit counselors. The services of credit counselors are often free. Credit counseling is widely offered on a volunteer basis; some corporations, universities, and city governments offer their services at no charge. There are also independent credit counselors, many of them accountants, who for a modest charge, generally $100 or $200, will help you get on the right track. The cost of these services is kept low because people seeking such services are generally experiencing financial difficulties.

Household management. A fully staffed household can cost as much as a fully staffed office. The household manager, who handles the supervision and hiring of other household employees, generally earns $30,000 per year or more.

The next highest paid employee is probably your cook. Full-time cook/chefs start at $500 a week, and more than a few make double that.

Nannies are much in demand and are often difficult to find in the United States. Those with proper experience and education start at $500 to $600 a week.

A housekeeper or maid with limited formal education, no cooking experience, and no child-care experience usually earns $60 per day. For that amount, most will take care of general housekeeping chores and laundry. Some will also handle household shopping.

"Senior caregivers" receive salaries close to those of nannies.

All of the salaries quoted here are for full-time employees; most people get by with part-time help. Many professional women, for example, have a housekeeper one or two days a week, a nanny to watch the children after school, and a cook to prepare food for business entertaining.

Having a household manager is a real luxury that is likely to be available only to those women who are running a household, orchestrating heavy business entertaining, raising one or more children, putting in long hours at the office and in business travel, and possibly caring for an aging parent (probably without the assistance of a husband).

Live-in help may be as much as one-third cheaper than live-out help, because you provide room and board in exchange for a lower salary. There is, however, rarely any real savings for you because the cost of the room the person occupies probably exceeds whatever you manage to save in weekly salary (unless, of course, you have a spare room and bath already).

Psychotherapists. A wide variety of psychological therapy is available, and there is a wide range of prices attached to such services. Group psychology sessions may be priced as low as $10 to $20 an hour; licensed psychologists may charge $75 per hour, and experienced psychiatrists charge anywhere from $75 to $200 per session.

Personal or social secretaries. If your personal and professional schedule is very demanding, you may require the services of a full- or part-time personal/social secretary.

Personal secretaries are usually paid by the hour at a rate based on their experience and technical abilities. Thus, a former executive secretary who also has word processing skills might earn $15 per hour, while someone brought in simply to type envelopes might earn the minimum wage. Fees are, of course, extremely negotiable.

Travel agents. Travel agents work on a commission basis and are paid by hotels, airlines, and car rental agencies. You do not pay a travel agent directly. The amount of commission the agent receives depends on the cost of your total purchase.

Professional shoppers. Professional shoppers are employed by major department stores; their services are generally free to major customers who purchase a minimum quantity of goods (generally several thousand dollars) in the store each year.

The direct cost to the customer is technically zero. The only hidden cost may be the loss of the option of buying the goods of a less expensive store.

Professional shopping services are also available privately. For a fee of about $75 an hour, personal shoppers will shop a variety of stores for you and may be able to pick up bargains that you would miss if you were restricted to one store.

Fitness trainers. The services of a personal fitness trainer at a fitness club or facility may cost as little as an extra $20 an hour. On the other hand, if you employ an independent fitness trainer who comes to your home, you can expect to pay anywhere from $50 to $100 per hour.

49

DIFFICULTIES WITH PROFESSIONAL ADVISERS

If you have a dispute with your investment adviser or stockbroker, you can take your complaint to the Securities and Exchange Commission Office of Consumer Affairs and Information Services, 450 Fifth Street, N.W., Washington, D.C.; to the National Association of Securities Dealers, Inc., Consumer Arbitration Center, Two World Trade Center, New York, New York 10048; or The Securities Investor Protection Corporation, 900 17th Street N.W., Washington, D.C. 20006.

If you have difficulties with your insurance broker or insurance company, you should contact the Health Insurance Association of America, 1850 K Street N.W., Washington, D.C. 20006; The American Council of Life Assurance at the same address; or The National Insurance Consumer Organization of Washington, D.C.

If you encounter a difficulty with your attorney, you might contact The American Bar Association Ethics Committee, New York, New York, or HALT (Help Abolish Legal Tyranny), 201 Massachusetts Avenue, N.E., Washington, D.C. 20002.

Civil rights violations. If you feel you have been discriminated against because of race, religion, sex, or marital status in any of your business dealings, you should contact the United States Commission on Civil Rights, 1121 Vermont Avenue N.W., Washington, D.C. 20425.

QUESTIONS AND ANSWERS

If you are happily employed, should you go on job interviews offered you by new prospective employers?

Yes. These interviews (even if you have initially no intention of accepting the position) provide good feedback regarding your current marketability.

Early in your career, should you always take the job that offers the greatest salary?

No. Early on, it's more important that you learn as much as possible and get as close to the center of power at your company as possible, so that you can see how the decision-making process works.

Another important consideration in *any* field is getting sales experience. It is always useful to have a stint in sales.

Is a stockbroker a financial planner?

Perhaps. Anyone can be a financial planner. Stockbrokers, bankers, insurance brokers, real estate brokers, and lawyers all can offer financial planning. The difficulty is that if the advice is tied to the particular service planner sells, it is not as pure as that which comes from a certified financial planner who is not trying to sell you a product.

When is it better to rent than to buy real estate?

It's more advantageous to rent if you do not expect to stay long in your present location or if your particular area is overbuilt and there is a depressed resale market for real estate but a lively rental market in which land-lords are offering special deals.

Can your employer change the structure of your health benefits?

Absolutely. Companies review the cost of health benefits every year. Because costs have increased dramatically, especially in recent years, the general trend is to greatly reduce the benefits offered and/or raise the contribution required from the employee.

How much life insurance do you need?

If you are head of your household, the rule of thumb is that you require an amount equal to twice your current annual salary. Individual situations, of course, require special review.

Will a travel agent always offer you the cheapest possible transportation and accommodations?

No, not necessarily, unless you ask for it. Travel agents work on a commission, and the more you spend, the more they make. All good travel agents offer you a range of possibilities and leave the final selection to you.

Is the cost of your fitness program tax deductible?

Possibly. If your doctor certifies in writing that you are required to have certain athletic equipment or physical therapy, at least a portion of your cost is probably tax deductible.

If you run your own business and you live with someone to whom you are not married, does this other person have any rights to your business?

Possibly. This is a gray area, with little precedent. However, if the other person has contributed to the formation and perhaps the day-to-day running of your business, he may have some legal claim.

How much should you save?

Starting with your very first paycheck, you should save a minimum of 5 percent of your gross pay. If you do this for a lifetime, the impact of compound interest will be enormous, and you will have a sizable nest egg upon retirement or when you need extra money for college tuition or possibly health care.

What will an executor do?

Your executor is responsible for administering your estate upon your death, according to your wishes. The executor will be required to pay outstanding bills, deal with insurance companies, and possibly sell real estate or even your own business. Your executor will contact your former employer to see to it that your heirs receive benefits due them. Finally, your executor will make sure that bequests, which you have made to various people, are properly carried out. If you have put funds in trust, the executor will handle the long-term payout rather than making a lump sum bequest to a beneficiary. The role of executor is difficult, tiring, and critical.

When should you start planning your retirement?

You should start planning your retirement as soon as you receive your first paycheck. It's good to develop the habit of saving at least five percent of your gross pay. This should be kept liquid until you amass enough to cover three months of living expenses. After that it should be invested conservatively for the long-range payout.

What is your investment risk tolerance?

To determine your risk tolerance, ask yourself how much of your life savings you are willing to risk on the outside chance of a higher return than that which you receive in conservative investments. If you are comfortable with only fifty percent of your investments in a conservative or even liquid state, then presumably you can stand the tension of knowing you could lose the whole other fifty percent.

If on the other hand, you have little or no risk tolerance, don't pretend you do. Invest everything conservatively so that you stay ahead of inflation and earn a decent return, one that you can depend on.

How much debt can you handle?

In difficult economic times, something close to zero is best (aside from your mortgage of course). Even in good times, it is not wise to get committed to anything beyond twenty percent of your net annual income.

Should you have a pre-nuptial or post-nuptial agreement?

Absolutely. Be realistic. Protect yourself. Avoid the possibility of expensive and drawn-out litigation at a later date.

Is real estate a sure thing?

No. In addition to economic ups and downs, there is the inescapable fact that housing built for the baby boomers does not have a ready market. The baby bust right behind the baby boom does not provide enough buyers for all of the baby boomers who want to sell their houses. Buy with great caution.

Can you hope to make a lifetime career in one company?

It is highly unlikely. Corporate America is undergoing enormous change—downsizing, merging, and repositioning. Many industries that have been the backbone of American employment are folding and being replaced by others which in many cases are far less stable.

GLOSSARY

alimony Payments made to a former spouse pursuant to divorce agreement.

annuities Policies that, at maturity, provide either a lump sum pay-out or periodic payments to a retiree or another beneficiary of the policy.

appreciation An increase in the value of an asset beyond original cost.

annual percentage rate (APR) The total interest cost to you of any loan or credit, calculated as a percentage of the amount borrowed.

asset Anything you own that is of value, such as a bank account, a house, stocks and bonds.

balance sheet The format listing all assets and all liabilities that you used to determine your net worth.

bankruptcy There are two types of bankruptcy—voluntary and involuntary. Voluntary Bankruptcy is a proceeding that you, the debtor, file in court. Involuntary Bankruptcy occurs when your creditors file a petition in court asking that you be declared bankrupt.

beneficiary The recipient of assets through enforcement of a trust, insurance policy, or will.

bond An interest-bearing security, issued by a private corporation or by a government.

broker A person who, for a commission or a fee, handles transactions between a buyer and seller, such as those involving real estate, insurance, stocks, and bonds.

collateral Property, or a pledge to that property, turned over by you to a borrower to secure funds you are borrowing.

compound interest An arrangement whereby interest is based on principal as well as on previous interest paid.

credit line The amount up to which a lending institution will permit you to borrow.

credit rating A determination by credit reporting agencies regarding the amount and type of credit you are able to carry.

discretionary income Income left after you have covered basic living expenses.

diversification The use of a variety of investments to spread risk.

dividends Payments to stockholders, set by the board of directors of a company, based on the earnings per share.

employee stock option plan (ESOP) Programs through which employees may purchase their company's stock at advantageous price.

equity The value of an asset less any debt existing against it.

equitable distribution A court-ordered disposition of jointly-held property after divorce—not necessarily equally.

executor The party responsible for disposition of your estate.

126

inflation The increase in your cost of living, including price increases that reduce the purchasing power of your dollars.

Keogh plan Retirement plans for those who are self-employed.

leverage Use of borrowed funds to acquire an investment.

liability Anything you owe, such as a mortgage or taxes.

limited partner An investor in a business who is liable only for the amount invested and who has no operating authority.

liquidity Those of your assets that are readily convertible to cash.

origination fee The sum banks charge for handling the administrative aspects of your mortgage.

net worth Your total assets minus your total liabilities.

principal The original amount borrowed upon which interest is paid.

profit-sharing An employer plan that allows employees to share in the profits of the company.

stock A security representing a share of ownership in a company. Preferred stock usually pays a fixed dividend. Common stock dividends may vary with the success of the company.

zero-coupon bonds Bonds on which interest accumulates annually but on which interest is not paid out until maturity. Unless these are part of an IRA or Keogh, you do have to pay taxes on the interest annually.

INDEX

130

More selected BARRON'S titles:

DICTIONARY OF COMPUTER TERMS, 2nd EDITION
Douglas Downing and Michael Covington
Nearly 1,000 computer terms are clearly explained, and sample
programs included. Paperback, $8.95, Canada $11.95/ISBN 4152-6,
288 pages

DICTIONARY OF FINANCE AND INVESTMENT TERMS,
3rd EDITION, *John Downs and Jordan Goodman*
Defines and explains over 3000 Wall Street terms for professionals,
business students, and average investors.
Paperback $9.95, Canada $13.95/ISBN 4631-5, 544 pages

DICTIONARY OF INSURANCE TERMS, 2nd EDITION
Harvey W. Rubin
Approximately 3000 insurance terms are defined as they relate to
property, casualty, life, health, and other types of insurance.
Paperback, $9.95, Canada $13.95/ISBN 4632-3, 416 pages

DICTIONARY OF REAL ESTATE TERMS, 2nd EDITION
Jack P. Friedman, Jack C. Harris, and Bruce Lindeman
Defines over 1200 terms, with examples and illustrations. A key
reference for everyone in real estate. Comprehensive and current.
Paperback $9.95, Canada $13.95/ISBN 3898-3, 224 pages

ACCOUNTING HANDBOOK, *Joel G. Siegel and Jae K. Shim*
Provides accounting rules, guidelines, formulas and techniques etc. to
help students and business professionals work out accounting problems.
Hardcover: $24.95, Canada $33.95/ISBN 6176-4, 832 pages

REAL ESTATE HANDBOOK, 2nd EDITION
Jack P. Friedman and Jack C. Harris
A dictionary/reference for everyone in real estate. Defines over 1500
legal, financial, and architectural terms.
Hardcover, $21.95, Canada $29.95/ISBN 5758-9, 700 pages

HOW TO PREPARE FOR REAL ESTATE LICENSING
EXAMINATIONS-SALESPERSON AND BROKER, 4th EDITION
Bruce Lindeman and Jack P. Friedman
Reviews current exam topics and features updated model exams and
supplemental exams, all with explained answers.
Paperback, $10.95, Canada $14.95/ISBN 4355-3, 340 pages

BARRON'S FINANCE AND INVESTMENT HANDBOOK,
3rd EDITION, *John Downes and Jordan Goodman*
This hard-working handbook of essential information defines more
than 3000 key terms, and explores 30 basic investment opportunities.
The investment information is thoroughly up-to-date. Hardcover $26.95,
Canada $36.95/ISBN 6188-8, approx. 1152 pages

FINANCIAL TABLES FOR MONEY MANAGEMENT
Stephen S. Solomon, Dr. Clifford Marshall, Martin Pepper,
Jack P. Friedman and Jack C. Harris
Pocket-sized handbooks of interest and investment rates tables used
easily by average investors and mortgage holders. Paperback
Savings and Loans, $6.95, Canada $9.95/ISBN 2745-0, 272 pages
Real Estate Loans, $6.95, Canada $9.95/ISBN 2744-2, 336 pages
Mortgage Payments, $5.95, Canada $8.50/ISBN 2728-0, 304 pages
Stocks and Bonds, $5.50, Canada $7.95/ISBN 2727-2, 256 pages
Comprehensive Annuities, $5.50, Canada $7.95/ISBN 2726-4, 160 pages
Canadian Mortgage Payments, Canada $9.95/ISBN 3939-4, 336 pages
Adjustable Rate Mortgages, $5.95, Canada $8.50/ISBN 3764-2, 288 pages

All prices are in U.S. and Canadian dollars and subject to change without notice.
At your bookseller, or order direct adding 10% postage (minimum charge $1.75,
Canada $2.00), N.Y. residents add sales tax.   ISBN PREFIX: 0-8120

Barron's Educational Series, Inc.
250 Wireless Boulevard, Hauppauge, NY 11788
Call toll-free: 1-800-645-3476, in NY 1-800-257-5729
In Canada: Georgetown Book Warehouse
34 Armstrong Ave., Georgetown, Ontario L7G 4R9
Call toll-free: 1-800-247-7160

More selected BARRON'S titles:

DICTIONARY OF ACCOUNTING TERMS
Siegel and Shim
Nearly 2500 terms related to accounting are defined.
Paperback, $9.95, Can. $13.95 (3766-9)

DICTIONARY OF ADVERTISING AND DIRECT MAIL TERMS
Imber and Toffler
Nearly 3000 terms used in the ad industry are defined.
Paperback, $9.95, Can. $13.95 (3765-0)

DICTIONARY OF BANKING TERMS
Fitch
Nearly 3000 terms related to banking, finance and money
management.
Paperback, $10.95, Can. $14.95 (3946-7)

DICTIONARY OF BUSINESS TERMS
Friedman, general editor
Over 6000 entries define business terms.
Paperback, $9.95, Can. $13.95 (3775-8)

BARRON'S BUSINESS REVIEW SERIES
These guides explain topics covered in a college-level business
course.
Each book: paperback

ACCOUNTING, 2nd EDITION. *Eisen.* $11.95, Can. $15.95 (4375-8)
BUSINESS LAW, *Hardwicke and Emerson.* $11.95, Can. $15.95 (3495-3)
BUSINESS STATISTICS, *Downing and Clark.* $11.95, Can. $15.95 (3576-3)
ECONOMICS, *Wessels.* $10.95, Can. $14.95 (3560-7)
FINANCE, 2nd EDITION. *Groppelli and Nikbakht.* $11.95,
Can. $15.95 (4373-1)
MANAGEMENT, *Montana and Charnov.* $11.95, Can. $15.50 (3559-3)
MARKETING, *Sandhusen.* $11.95, Can. $15.50 (3494-5)
QUANTITATIVE METHODS, *Downing and Clark.* $10.95,
Can. $14.95 (3947-5)

TALKING BUSINESS SERIES: BILINGUAL DICTIONARIES
Five bilingual dictionaries translate about 3000 terms not found in
most foreign phrasebooks.
Each book: paperback

TALKING BUSINESS IN FRENCH, *Le Gal.* $9.95, Can. $13.95
(3745-6)
TALKING BUSINESS IN GERMAN, *Strutz.* $9.95, Can. $12.95
(3747-2)
TALKING BUSINESS IN ITALIAN, *Rakus.* $8.95, Can. $11.95
(3754-5)
TALKING BUSINESS IN JAPANESE, *C. Akiyama and N. Akiyama.*
$9.95, Can. $12.95 (3848-7)
TALKING BUSINESS IN KOREAN, *Cheong.* $8.95, Can. $11.95
(3992-0)
TALKING BUSINESS IN SPANISH, *Fryer and Faria.* $9.95,
Can. $13.95 (3769-3)

All prices are in U.S. and Canadian dollars and subject to change without notice.
At your bookseller, or order direct adding 10% postage (minimum charge $1.75,
Canada $2.00), N.Y. residents add sales tax.   ISBN PREFIX: 0-8120

Barron's Educational Series, Inc.
250 Wireless Boulevard, Hauppauge, NY 11788
Call toll-free: 1-800-645-3476, in NY 1-800-257-5729
In Canada: Georgetown Book Warehouse
34 Armstrong Ave., Georgetown, Ontario L7G 4R9
Call toll-free: 1-800-247-7160

BARRON'S BUSINESS KEYS Each "key" explains 50 important concepts and contains a glossary and index. Each book: Paperback, 160 pp., 4³/₁₆″ × 7″, $4.95, Can. $6.50. ISBN Prefix: 0-8120

Titles include:

Keys for Women Starting or Owning a Business (4609-9)
Keys to Business and Personal Financial Statements (4622-6)
Keys to Buying a Franchise (4484-3)
Keys to Buying and Owning a Home (4251-4)
Keys to Buying and Selling a Business (4430-4)
Keys to Estate Planning and Trusts (4188-7)
Keys to Filing for Bankruptcy (4383-9)
Keys to Financing a College Education (4468-1)
Keys to Improving Your ROI (4641-2)
Keys to Incorporating (3973-4)
Keys to Investing in Common Stocks (4291-3)
Keys to Investing in Corporate Bonds (4386-3)
Keys to Investing in Government Securities (4485-1)
Keys to Investing in Mutual Funds (4162-3)
Keys to Investing in Options and Futures (4481-9)
Keys to Investing in Real Estate (3928-9)
Keys to Mortgage Financing and Refinancing (4219-0)
Keys to Personal Financial Planning (4537-8)
Keys to Purchasing a Condo or a Co-op (4218-2)
Keys to Reading an Annual Report (3930-0)
Keys to Retirement Planning (4230-1)
Keys to Risks and Rewards of Penny Stocks (4300-6)
Keys to Saving Money on Income Taxes (4467-3)
Keys to Starting a Small Business (4487-8)
Keys to Surviving a Tax Audit (4513-0)
Keys to Understanding the Financial News (4206-9)
Keys to Understanding Securities (4229-8)
Keys to Women's Basic Professional Needs (4608-0)

Books may be purchased at your bookstore, or by mail from Barron's. Enclose check or money order for total amount plus sales tax where applicable and 10% for postage and handling (minimum charge $1.75, Canada $2.00). Prices subject to change without notice.

Barron's Educational Series, Inc.
250 Wireless Blvd., Hauppauge, NY 11788
Call toll-free: 1-800-645-3476, in NY: 1-800-257-5729
In Canada: Georgetown Book Warehouse
34 Armstrong Ave., Georgetown, Ont. L7G 4R9
Call toll-free: 1-800-247-7160